ICE CREAM

by
Mable & Gar Hoffman

ANOTHER BEST-SELLING VOLUME FROM HPBooks®

Publisher: Rick Bailey; Editorial Director: Elaine Woodard
Editor: Carroll Latham; Art Director: Don Burton
Typography: Cindy Coatsworth, Joanne Nociti, Michelle Carter
Director of Manufacturing: Anthony B. Narducci
Research Assistant: Jan Robertson; Food Stylist: Mable Hoffman
Photography: George de Gennaro Studios.

Published by HPBooks, Inc.
P.O. Box 5367, Tucson, AZ 85703   602/888-2150
ISBN 0-89586-040-6   Library of Congress Catalog Card Number 81-80744
©1981 HPBooks, Inc.   Printed in U.S.A.
5th Printing

Cover photo: Old Fashioned Strawberry Ice Cream, page 36
On previous pages, Classic Banana Split, page 145

Table of Contents

The Ice Cream Story 6
Making Ice Cream 10
Definitions of Frozen Desserts 16
Vanilla 18
Chocolate, Coffee & Tea 24
Fruits of the Vine 35
Citrus Fruits 50
Orchard Fruits 62
Tropical Fruits 79
Melons & Vegetables 93
Pies & Cakes 101
Just For Kids 112
Nuts, Candies & Caramels 121
Molded Frozen Desserts 131
Soda Fountain & Bar Concoctions 144

The Ice Cream Story

On returning from a voyage to the Orient, Marco Polo reported seeing Chinese ices made with milk. The Romans served frozen fruit ices but after the return of Marco Polo, the use of ices made with milk and cream spread throughout Europe and Asia. Until the early 1800's its enjoyment was confined to heads of state and nobility. In 1809, Dolly Madison, wife of the President of the United States, first served ice cream to dinner guests at the White House. Thus she became known as the first lady of ice cream in America.

Until the invention of mechanical refrigeration, ice cream was stored in large, heavily insulated boxes inside bulky metal containers filled with a salt-and-ice mixture called *brine*. These brine containers held the temperature inside the storage box below freezing. If salt and ice were not replenished daily, the temperature rose above freezing and disaster followed. Only commercial firms and the very affluent could afford the luxury of storing ice cream.

About 1900, ice cream makers were developed for home use. With readily available commercial ice cream and the introduction of homemade ice cream, it was natural for it to become a favorite dessert.

Following the invention of electric home refrigerators, freezer compartments were developed and gradually enlarged and improved. It was then possible to make and store ice cream and frozen desserts at home. Drudgery of hand cranking was largely eliminated with the introduction of electric-powered ice cream makers. However, there are still those who insist no other method will duplicate the flavor of hand-cranked ice cream.

Frozen dessert flavors have increased from chocolate, vanilla and strawberry to include exotic tropical flavors and a variety of exciting combinations. Today, most frozen desserts are easy to make and even tropical ingredients are readily available in supermarkets. They can be frozen by *churning* them in an ice cream maker or they can be *still-frozen* in a freezer.

There are many advantages to making your own frozen desserts. You can enjoy beautifully molded *bombes*, tangy *yogurt* confections, delicious *ices* and a wide variety of ice creams at about half the cost of commercially produced frozen desserts. You know ingredients are fresh and pure because you purchase them immediately before creating your frozen dessert. You can control or eliminate most chemical emulsifiers, stabilizers and artificial flavors that are found in most commercial products. Many more flavors are available than can be found in any commercial establishment. And homemade frozen desserts can be stored in the freezer and enjoyed anytime.

We hope this book encourages you to make and enjoy frozen desserts frequently. Serve them with confidence that your guests will be delighted.

Selecting An Ice Cream Maker

Refering to the picture to the right, most ice cream makers have (1) a manual or electric-powered crank-and-gear assembly, (2) a lid, (3) a dasher, (4) an ice cream canister and (5) an ice bucket. The crank-and-gear assembly sits on top of the canister and bucket and turns the canister. The canister rotates while immersed in a brine solution in the ice bucket. The dasher extends from top to bottom of the canister and remains stationary. It scrapes tiny frozen ice crystals from inside the canister and distributes them throughout the mixture.

In the past, most ice cream makers made 1 to 1-1/2 gallons at a time. Now there are counter-top ice cream makers with 1- and 2-quart capacities. All are powered by an electric motor under, rather than on top of the ice bucket. They have some significant advantages: the brine solution can be made with table salt and whole ice cubes; they are relatively light-weight and can be operated on a kitchen counter; you can make small quantities for small families; transparent or translucent canister lids let you watch the ice cream as it freezes. There are three ice cream makers which use no brine. In one, the entire machine is placed in your freezer. The motor generates heat which increases the temperature in the freezer. This lengthens the freezing process significantly. The others are self-refrigerated, electric ice cream makers used on countertops. Only one has a timer. Both make about 5 cups of ice cream.

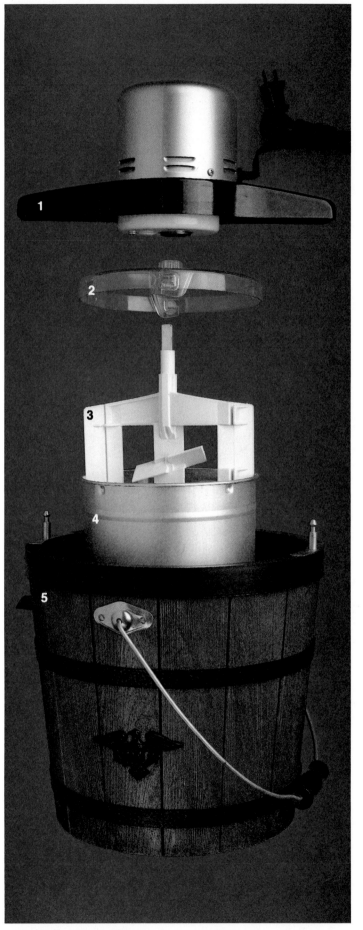

Parts of Ice Cream Maker

Size is one of the most important considerations in selecting an ice cream maker. They come in 1-, 2-, 4- and 6-quart sizes. It is better to buy one with a large canister than to make several batches. You can make small amounts in a large canister or make the full amount and store what isn't eaten for later enjoyment. To choose among them, consider your family's size and its appetite for ice cream.

Deciding between a hand-cranked or motor-driven machine is easy. If you always have plenty of eager helpers with strong arms to provide cranking power, buy the hand-cranked model. They usually cost less than electric-powered ice cream makers. On the other hand, if cost is not important and the cranking chore usually is done by you, buy the motor-driven model. Relax while the hard work is done for you.

Consider the ice bucket construction. Wood, although more expensive than plastic or fiberglass, has better insulating qualities which reduce the salt and ice used. Wood is also less likely to crack or break. If not used frequently, wooden buckets often must be soaked in water several hours. As it soaks up water, the wood swells and becomes leakproof. Plastic and fiberglass are ready to use at a moment's notice.

Care of Ice Cream Maker

Wash the canister, lid and dasher with hot soapy water *before and after* each use. Then thoroughly rinse and dry them. This inhibits rusting of metal parts. Fortunately, many parts are made of plastic and/or metal alloys and are somewhat immune to the corrosive effects of salt water. However, salt water very quickly rusts any unprotected metal parts of the hand crank, gear housing and ice bucket fittings. These should be hosed down with fresh water after each use. ***Do not hose down electric motors and their gear housings.*** Wipe away salt residue on the motor and gear housing with a damp cloth or sponge. If you are a believer in preventive maintenance, occasionally apply a metal preservative or wax to the metal parts.

CAUTION! If your machine is electrically powered, always disconnect the cord from the electrical outlet before attempting to empty or clean it. Never immerse the motor and gear housing in water or spray with water.

Source & Preparation of Ice

Water frozen in used milk cartons is the most economical and convenient source of ice. Nine half-gallon milk cartons occupy less than one cubic foot of freezer space, yet provide as much ice as 34 average-size ice cube trays. This is enough ice to freeze and *ripen* or harden six quarts of ice cream or make three batches of ice cream in a 2-quart ice cream maker. Wash empty milk cartons with hot soapy water and rinse them thoroughly. Fill quart containers 3/4 inch from the top with water; fill 1/2-gallon containers 1-1/2 inches from the top. Close the carton and tape securely with plastic tape or freezer tape. Store upright in your freezer until frozen solid, then rearrange cartons for more efficient use of

How to Prepare Ice _____

1/Fill clean unbroken half-gallon milk cartons 1-1/2 inches from top with tap water. Close and seal tops. Freeze in upright position.

freezer space. Each half-gallon container yields 3-3/4 pounds of ice. By contrast, an average ice cube tray yields only 1 pound.

To use ice frozen in milk cartons, lay cartons on concrete or another hard surface. Using a hammer or the blunt end of an axe, strike the sides and bottom of each carton four or five times to break the ice into small pieces. Cartons should not be heavily damaged but may have small holes in them. Crushed ice the size of cherries is ideal for freezing ice cream. However, slightly larger or smaller pieces have no significant effect on the quality of the finished ice cream.

Ready-to-use crushed ice in 10- and 20-pound bags is available in most supermarkets. Block ice is perhaps the least convenient to use in ice cream making but is readily available in some communities. Use an ice pick to reduce large blocks to smaller, more manageable chunks for crushing.

To crush chunks of ice, place in a large, clean, heavy fabric purse, burlap bag, large piece of canvas or other heavy flexible material. Close the top if possible, then pound with a wooden 2'' x 4'' or broad side of a hammer or axe until crushed to desired size.

Alternately pour crushed ice and salt around the filled canister inside the ice bucket. Unless your ice cream maker is made especially to accommodate whole ice cubes, crush them.

2/Lay ice in cartons on a hard surface. With hammer, axe or wooden mallet, strike side and bottom 4 or 5 times until ice is crushed.

3/Open top of carton and pour crushed ice alternately with salt into ice bucket. Half-gallon cartons contain about 3-3/4 pounds of ice.

Making Ice Cream

For clarity, the term *ice cream maker* is used throughout this book when referring to a mechanical hand-cranked or electric-powered ice cream freezer in which mixtures are *churn-frozen*. *Freezer* refers to the freezer compartment of a refrigerator-freezer, a free-standing box or upright freezer where mixtures are *still-frozen*.

Mixtures may be frozen in an ice cream maker or in a freezer. To freeze in an ice cream maker, pour the mixture into the metal canister. Insert the canister in the ice bucket and attach the crank system to the top. The canister is rotated by a hand crank or electric motor. A salt-and-ice mixture or *brine* (see Preparing the Brine, next page) is poured around the canister. This *churn method* usually produces a much smoother finished product than when still-frozen in a freezer.

When using the *still-freeze method*, pour the ice cream mixture into a loaf pan, square baking pan or several undivided ice cube trays. Place the mixture and container in the freezer. Because there is no agitation during freezing, large ice crystals usually form. To minimize ice crystal formation, stir or beat the mixture two or three times during the freezing process. Or break the mixture into pieces and beat with a mixer or food processor just prior to serving. The type of agitation recommended varies with the kinds of ingredients. Follow directions given with each recipe. Many mixtures frozen in freezers contain whipping cream, eggs, cornstarch, gelatin or marshmallows. When added at the proper time and in the proper way, these ingredients help reduce the formation of large ice crystals.

How to Freeze Ice Cream

1/With dasher in ice cream canister, pour ice cream mixture into canister to fill line.

2/Place lid on canister. Insert filled canister into empty ice bucket.

Preparing the Brine

Salt-to-ice ratio determines brine temperature and thus the temperature at which the ice cream will be frozen. If there is too much salt, the ice cream will freeze too quickly and will be grainy or have large ice crystals. If there is too little salt or the ice cream mixture is too warm when churning begins, it will freeze too slowly, resulting in a soft and sometimes buttery mixture. Time required to freeze an ice cream mixture is influenced by the sugar, butterfat and milk solid content of the ingredients, ice bucket insulating qualities, temperature of the ice cream mixture, atmospheric temperature and several other conditions. With all these factors affecting the freezing process, it is impossible to provide a single, ideal salt-to-ice ratio. Our experience confirmed that *table salt* works well with whole ice cubes because the small salt granules rapidly melt relatively large pieces of ice. *Rock salt*, which dissolves more slowly, is more efficient with crushed ice. We found the following to be the most successful:

Ratios of Salt to Ice:

1-1/2 cups table salt combined with six pounds whole ice cubes

1 cup rock salt combined with six pounds crushed ice

Use these ratios to begin freezing ice cream. *Increase* salt to lower the brine temperature and shorten processing time. Also increase salt content slightly when the ice cream mixture is above average in sugar content or contains an alcoholic beverage. *Decrease* salt to raise brine temperature and lengthen processing time. Decrease salt content slightly when the ice cream mixture is relatively low in sugar content or high in butterfat content.

3/Secure top or motor-and-gear assembly on top of ice bucket and canister.

4/Fill bucket with ice cubes and table salt or crushed ice and rock salt in alternate layers.

Ripening Ice Cream

Ice cream is usually consumed immediately after it's frozen. Many people prefer to *ripen* or harden the mixture before serving. *Ripening* firms the ice cream and allows flavors to blend. Molded frozen desserts are always ripened. If you plan to mold ice cream into an interesting shape, it must be hard enough to retain the shape of the mold when served.

To ripen ice cream in the freezer, remove the canister from the ice cream maker and wipe the outside with a cloth or sponge to remove any salt and ice. Plug the dasher hole or cover the canister with foil and place it in the freezer. Freeze one to three hours until the mixture is firm. If your shelves will not hold the canister, spoon the mixture into another container with a tight-fitting lid.

Ice cream can also be ripened in the brine. As soon as it becomes extremely difficult to turn the crank or the motor slows down, remove the crank-and-gear housing or electric motor and housing. Remove any brine mixture covering the lid and spoon off the brine mixture to about one inch below the top of the ice cream canister. Wipe the canister lid with a damp cloth to prevent salt from falling into the frozen mixture. Gently remove the canister lid. Holding the canister in the ice bucket with one hand, gently but firmly pull out the dasher. Hold the dasher directly above the canister while scraping ice cream from the dasher into the canister. Set the dasher aside. Scrape down the inside of the canister with a wooden spoon and stir the ice cream briefly to release any air bubbles left by removing the dasher. Stirring will distribute any nuts, candy or marshmallows. Lay a double layer of waxed paper over the top of the canister. Replace the lid and put a cork or ball of foil into the dasher hole. Cover the lid with a large plastic bag or piece of heavy foil. Hold the canister in place while tipping the ice bucket far enough to drain off most of the salt water through the drain hole. Return the

How to Ripen Ice Cream

1/Holding canister in place, gently pull dasher from frozen ice cream. Spoon ice cream from dasher back into canister.

2/Place lid on ice cream canister. Insert cork or crumbled foil into hole and cover lid with foil or a plastic bag.

bucket to its upright position. With a long kitchen tool or stick, tamp down the ice and salt left in the ice bucket. Fill the ice bucket about one inch above the canister lid with a brine mixture, using one cup of salt to three pounds of ice. Cover the canister and bucket with a folded towel or blanket or several thicknesses of newspaper for insulation. Let ripen one to three hours before serving.

Enjoy homemade ice cream on a picnic or tailgate party by packing it in brine before leaving home. Be sure the ice cream maker is placed so it can't possibly overturn. Should such a disaster happen, rinse everything immediately and thoroughly with water or the inside of your car will be sure to rust.

Serving Ice Cream

One quart of ice cream or frozen dessert will serve six to eight persons. Plan eight to ten servings per quart when served as an accompaniment to other desserts such as pie or cake a la mode. When serving teenagers, cut the above yields in half or be prepared for complaints.

Ice cream and frozen desserts should be slightly softened and pliable before serving. If frozen too solid, they have a tendency to move about on the plate, making it difficult to eat. This can be inconvenient at best, but downright embarrassing when pieces suddenly fly off the plate. If frozen desserts become too soft, the great pleasures of firm, cold, delicious ice cream are lost. To keep the frozen mixture from clinging to them, occasionally dip scooping and cutting utensils into cold tap water.

Check the firmness of your frozen dessert about one hour before serving time. If it is still very soft, lower the freezer compartment temperature. If it is too hard, raise the temperature in the freezer compartment or place molded ice creams in the refrigerator 10 to 15 minutes before serving. The quickest and best way to soften still-frozen ice cream, ices, sherbets and sorbets, is to process them in a food processor until fluffy but not thawed. Use the metal blade. This method cannot be used for molded frozen desserts.

3/Holding ice cream canister in bucket, carefully tilt bucket and pour off most of the salt water through drain hole.

4/Fill bucket with brine mixture of 3 pounds ice to 1 cup salt. Cover with towels or newspapers to insulate.

Storing Ice Cream

Let's face it—homemade ice cream and frozen desserts are at their best when eaten within three hours of their preparation. Because they contain little or no stabilizers, their storage life is shorter than commercial ice cream. For best quality and flavor, we recommend homemade ice cream be kept no longer than two weeks.

Use containers with tight-fitting lids to store homemade ice cream and frozen desserts in a freezer. This is especially important with a frost-free freezer. The same process which removes moisture from the freezer compartment also removes moisture from unprotected or poorly protected foods. Ice cream should be stored at 10° to 0°F (-10° to -20°C). At these temperatures, ice cream will be firm, yet pliable. It should be neither mushy nor too firm to serve.

Cover molded ice cream, pies and cakes with foil or plastic wrap while they are ripening in a freezer. If they will be held in the freezer longer than 8 to 10 hours, wrap them and their containers in foil, making airtight packages. Or place in freezer bags that can be tightly closed. This will prevent the formation of large ice crystals. Place ice cream sandwiches and bonbons in rigid containers such as baking pans or small boxes. Wrap tightly in foil or seal in freezer bags.

Ingredients

Milk is the basic ingredient in most ice creams. When a recipe calls for milk, use *fresh whole homogenized-pasteurized milk.* Like all fresh dairy products, milk should be refrigerated at all times.

Skim milk, also called *non-fat milk,* contains little or no fat. It is used in low-calorie recipes.

Evaporated milk is more concentrated than whole fresh milk, giving a richer taste and smoother texture to ice cream. When diluted with equal parts of water, it may be used as a substitute for whole milk. We prefer to use it undiluted as it comes from the can.

Sweetened condensed milk should not be confused with evaporated milk. It is a concentrated milk with a large amount of sugar added for flavor. Used undiluted, it makes a smooth texture and gives a unique flavor to ice cream. It does not require refrigeration before opening. However, if the mixture is a dark caramel color when opened, it has been subjected to heat or is old and will affect the color of the ice cream. Use only light-colored sweetened condensed milk.

Non-fat dry milk is economical and needs no refrigeration until it is reconstituted. It is available in supermarkets as *instant* dry milk granules or *non-instant* dry milk powder. Instant non-fat dry milk is easily reconstituted by stirring dry granules into water. Carefully mix non-instant dry milk with a small amount of water to make a paste before adding the remaining water.

Buttermilk is thicker and lower in calories than whole milk. Its slightly tart flavor is excellent in some ice creams and is a favorite with many people. Buttermilk often separates as it stands. Stir or shake it before using.

Half-and-half, as the name implies, is a mixture of milk and cream and is often called *light cream.* It provides limited richness to ice cream but is not heavy enough to be whipped.

Whipping cream is heavy and when whipped, traps air in tiny pockets. Unwhipped or whipped, it produces a smooth, very rich ice cream. When we use the term *whipping cream* in a recipe, we refer to unwhipped cream as it is poured from the carton. The term *whipped cream* is whipping cream that has already been whipped.

Dairy sour cream is found in the dairy section of supermarkets. Its slightly tart flavor and smooth, thick texture make it an ideal ice cream ingredient.

Yogurt is available both unflavored and in a wide variety of fruit flavors. Stir yogurt with a spoon or whisk before combining with other ingredients. Its slightly tart flavor adds interest to frozen desserts.

Eggs are one of the most important ingredients in ice cream. They serve as a thickening agent for custard-type mixtures and provide a light texture when air is beaten into them. Recipes in this book were tested with large eggs. When asked to *beat eggs slightly,* use a fork, spoon or whisk to beat whites and yolks together until blended into one color. When we use the term *beat until thick and lemon-colored,* beat eggs with an electric mixer four or five minutes. Eggs are often *separated* for use in frozen desserts. Although easier to separate when cold, egg whites at room temperature beat to a larger volume. After you separate the cold egg, let the egg white stand at room temperature at least 10 minutes. Beat egg whites until soft

Clockwise from top: Strawberry Soda, page 146; in glass dish: Cherry-Berry Sorbet, page 66, Tangerine Sorbet, page 61, Lemon Ice, page 56 and Strawberry Sorbet, page 41; Old-Fashioned Vanilla Ice Cream, page 20, with Favorite Fudge Sauce, page 154.

peaks begin to form. Continue to beat while gradually adding sugar. Continue beating to the stage indicated in the recipe.

Sugar, when listed without any other description, refers to granulated sugar. It's the most popular type of sugar used to sweeten homemade ice cream and the one used most often in our recipes. Brown sugar is used for a butterscotch flavor or where it blends naturally with other foods. *Lightly pack* brown sugar by spooning sugar into a measuring cup, lightly pressing each spoonful into the cup with the back of the spoon until the required level is reached.

Honey provides a distinctive flavor. Depending on the source, there may be a slight orange, clover or sage flavor. Honey does not change the texture of ice cream.

Light corn syrup is used with sugar in many of the fruit ices, sherbets and sorbets. It gives a light, smooth texture without affecting flavors. *Dark corn syrup* is used for its distinctive flavor.

Maple syrup in these recipes is maple-flavored pancake syrup. Genuine maple syrup will give your ice cream a much richer maple flavor.

Unflavored gelatin contributes no flavor to ice cream. When dissolved and mixed with other ingredients, it assists in making a smooth texture. Each envelope contains about *one tablespoon* unflavored gelatin. Some recipes require only *one teaspoon* to make a very good product. Wherever this reduced amount of unflavored gelatin is used, *one teaspoon* is in italics.

Cornstarch is used in some of the cooked mixtures as a thickening agent and to help make a smooth product. Cook these mixtures the recommended length of time to eliminate the flavor of uncooked starch.

Marshmallows and marshmallow creme each have a gelatin base and a light texture. Including either of them will give your ice cream a smoother texture.

Flavorings range from vanilla and chocolate to berries, nuts, fruits, coffee and tea. When making any frozen dessert, use *pure vanilla extract,* not artificial vanilla flavoring or a blend. Artificial vanilla flavoring disappears when frozen. Read the individual chapter introductions for more detailed information on flavorings.

Definitions of Frozen Desserts

Ice Cream: Most of us use the term ice cream when referring to any frozen dessert. Actually, ice cream is a frozen mixture with a high fat content. It is rich with cream, milk, sweeteners and flavorings. Most homemade ice creams are actually French ice creams or frozen custards because they contain whole eggs or egg yolks.

Sherbets: Milk is used instead of cream in sherbets. They also contain fruits or fruit juices and sugar or another sweetener. Sherbets have a much lower fat content and are not as smooth and rich as ice creams. Unflavored gelatin or beaten egg whites are often added to give them a lighter, fluffier texture.

Sorbets: French sorbets are similar to American-style ices. They are frozen combinations of pureed fresh fruits, fruit juices and sweeteners. Some contain wines or liqueurs. They contain no milk or eggs to reduce ice crystals, and must be stirred during freezing. Or scrape the frozen mixture with a fork until the pieces resemble finely crushed ice. Sorbets take on a delightfully light and fluffy texture when beaten in a food processor with the metal blade. Sorbets are definitely at their best when eaten immediately after freezing.

Ices: These relatives of sorbets may be made with one or more pureed fruits or fruit juices and a sweetener. They must be stirred while freezing or the frozen mixture must be scraped with a fork or beaten in a food processor with the metal blade to break up ice crystals.

Frappés: Similar to ices, these mixtures are not frozen solid but are served while still slushy.

Frozen Yogurt: Plain or flavored yogurt is used instead of cream or milk. These sweetened mixtures usually include fruit or fruit juices. Yogurt gives a tangy flavor many people enjoy. In some recipes, cream is added to make a smoother, richer dessert.

Frozen Mousse: Rich in eggs and cream, this smooth mixture requires no stirring as it freezes. Beaten egg whites and whipped cream are folded into the custard-like base. The mixture is then frozen in a bowl or mold and unmolded before serving.

Frozen Soufflé: Similar to a mousse, this light, creamy mixture is frozen in a soufflé dish and is served directly from that dish.

Bombe: The name comes from a ridged, melon-shaped mold called a *bombe.* It is about the size of a cantaloupe. Bombes are usually layered with two or more kinds of ice cream.

Mable & Gar Hoffman

Mable and Gar Hoffman have enjoyed making ice cream ever since their childhoods in Maryland. As teen-agers both earned spending money in their local ice cream shops. For many years each had their own careers, Mable as a consulting home economist and Gar as a personnel manager. They have now combined their interests and talents. Together they own and manage Hoffman Food Consultants, Inc. They concentrate their efforts on food consulting, food styling, recipe development and writing.

Their continuous research for regional and ethnic cuisine has resulted in extensive travel throughout the world. Although Mable's name appears on most of their books, Gar has been a silent contributor. Their previous cookbooks published by HPBooks include *Appetizers, Chocolate Cookery, Mini Deep-Fry Cookery, Crepe Cookery* and *Crockery Cookery.* The last two mentioned have had spectacular success. Each was on the New York Times best-seller list several months and each won the R. T. French Tastemaker Award, the "Oscar" for softcover cookbooks.

Vanilla

What is the most popular ice cream flavor? Vanilla, of course. Most people enjoy the mild vanilla flavor without the contrast of fruits, chocolate or other ingredients. Others choose vanilla because it is compatible with almost any other flavor. It is delicious when served alone but becomes refreshing and different when decorated with a sauce or mixed with fruits or nuts.

Use fresh ingredients when making homemade ice cream. Look for the expiration date on milk, cream and egg cartons and buy the freshest. Use only *pure vanilla extract* when making frozen desserts. Imitation vanilla flavoring freezes out of mixtures leaving a weak, diluted taste.

If you like a mild vanilla flavor, you'll like Basic Vanilla Ice Cream. It is a rich mixture of milk and cream cooked with sugar and egg yolks. Whipping cream is added for extra smoothness and pure vanilla extract for rich flavor. Vanilla Ice Cream has similar ingredients but requires no cooking or cooling before it is frozen. For those who are allergic to eggs or want to cut down on egg consumption, Quick Vanilla Ice Cream contains no eggs and is simple to make.

Several recipes contain unflavored gelatin or undiluted evaporated milk for extra body and smoothness. Frozen Custard contains unflavored gelatin and is also rich with eggs and cream. You'll be delighted with its smooth texture and the rich creamy flavor. Old-Fashioned Vanilla Ice Cream, which contains undiluted evaporated milk, whole milk, egg yolks and cream, is not as rich, but is light, fluffy and very creamy. Make it by the freezer method if you like, but the texture is better when made in an ice cream maker. The results make the extra effort worthwhile.

Vanilla Ice Cream

Quick ice cream made without cooking.

2 eggs
1 cup sugar
2-3/4 cups half-and-half

1 tablespoon vanilla extract
1 cup whipping cream

In a large bowl, beat eggs until thick and lemon colored. Beat in sugar until light and fluffy. Stir in half-and-half, vanilla and whipping cream. Pour into ice cream canister. Freeze in ice cream maker according to manufacturer's directions. Makes about 2 quarts.

Basic Vanilla Ice Cream

Standard vanilla ice cream made by cooking eggs, sugar and cream before freezing.

3 cups half-and-half
1 cup sugar
4 egg yolks, well beaten

1 cup whipping cream
1 tablespoon vanilla extract

In a heavy medium saucepan, combine half-and-half, sugar and beaten egg yolks. Cook and stir over low heat until mixture coats a metal spoon and is slightly thickened. Cool to room temperature. Stir in whipping cream and vanilla. Pour into ice cream canister. Freeze in ice cream maker according to manufacturer's directions. Makes about 2 quarts.

Royal Crown Vanilla

Queen of the super-rich vanilla ice creams.

5 egg yolks
2/3 cup sugar
1 cup half-and-half

2 tablespoons butter
1 cup whipping cream
2 teaspoons vanilla extract

In a medium bowl, beat egg yolks and sugar until well blended. Pour into top of double boiler. Stir in half-and-half. Cook and stir over gently boiling water until mixture thickens. Set aside. Stir in butter. Stirring occasionally, cool on a rack to room temperature. Stir in whipping cream and vanilla. Pour into ice cream canister. Freeze in ice cream maker according to manufacturer's directions. Makes about 1 quart.

Old-Fashioned Vanilla Ice Cream

Photo on pages 15 and 117.

The Hoffman family's all-time favorite.

1-1/3 cups sugar
1 tablespoon cornstarch
1/4 teaspoon salt
3 cups whole milk

2 egg yolks
1 (5.33-oz.) can evaporated milk
1 cup whipping cream
1 tablespoon vanilla extract

In a medium saucepan, combine sugar, cornstarch and salt. Stir in whole milk. Stir over medium heat until mixture begins to simmer. Simmer 1 minute over low heat; set aside. In a small bowl, lightly beat egg yolks. Stir about 1 cup milk mixture into egg yolks; stir egg yolk mixture into remaining milk mixture. Cook and stir over low heat 2 minutes or until slightly thickened. Stir in evaporated milk, whipping cream and vanilla. Cool to room temperature. Pour into ice cream canister. Freeze in ice cream maker according to manufacturer's directions. Makes 2 quarts.

Soft Vanilla Ice Cream

Soft, smooth texture similar to commercial soft ice cream.

1 *teaspoon* unflavored gelatin
2 tablespoons cold water
2 cups whole milk
3/4 cup instant non-fat dry milk powder

1 cup sugar
2 cups whipping cream
1 tablespoon vanilla extract

In a medium saucepan, sprinkle gelatin over cold water to soften. Stir over very low heat until gelatin dissolves. Gradually stir in whole milk. Stir in dry milk powder and sugar. Stir in whipping cream and vanilla until blended. Pour into ice cream canister. Freeze in ice cream maker according to manufacturer's directions. Serve when mixture is firm enough to hold soft peaks. Makes about 2 quarts.

Quick Vanilla Ice Cream

Rich with cream but contains no eggs.

1 qt. half-and-half
1 cup sugar

1 tablespoon vanilla extract
2 cups whipping cream

In a large bowl, combine half-and-half and sugar, stirring until sugar dissolves. Stir in vanilla and whipping cream. Pour into ice cream canister. Freeze in ice cream maker according to manufacturer's directions. Makes about 2 quarts.

Old-Fashioned Vanilla Ice Cream in a Cone

Italian-Style Frozen Yogurt

A good basic frozen yogurt.

3/4 cup sugar
1/4 cup water
2 egg whites
1/8 teaspoon cream of tartar

2 cups plain yogurt
2 teaspoons vanilla extract
Chocolate syrup or fruit topping

In a small saucepan, combine sugar and water. Stir until mixture comes to a boil and sugar dissolves. Boil without stirring until syrup reaches 238°F (114°C) on a candy thermometer or syrup forms a soft ball when a small amount is dropped into cold water; set aside. In a medium bowl, beat egg whites and cream of tartar with electric mixer until soft peaks form. Beating constantly, immediately pour hot syrup in a thin stream over beaten egg whites. Continue beating until cool and thick; set aside. In a large bowl, stir yogurt until smooth. Stir in vanilla. Gradually fold egg white mixture into yogurt. Spoon into a 9" x 5" loaf pan or several undivided ice trays. Cover with foil or plastic wrap. Place in freezer; freeze until firm, 3 to 6 hours. Serve with chocolate syrup or fruit topping. Makes about 1 quart.

Calorie-Counter's Ice Cream

For extra calorie and money savings, make the milk from non-fat milk powder.

1/2 cup sugar
2 tablespoons cornstarch
1/8 teaspoon salt
5 cups skim milk or low-fat milk

1/2 cup light corn syrup
2 eggs
1 tablespoon vanilla extract

In a medium saucepan, combine sugar, cornstarch and salt. Gradually stir in milk and corn syrup. Cook and stir over low heat until mixture is slightly thickened; set aside. In a small bowl, beat eggs. Stir about 1 cup hot milk mixture into beaten eggs. Stir egg mixture into remaining milk mixture. Stir over low heat until bubbly, 4 to 5 minutes. Cool to room temperature; stir in vanilla. Pour into ice cream canister. Freeze in ice cream maker according to manufacturer's directions. Makes about 2 quarts.

If you prefer a less rich ice cream, substitute equal amounts of regular milk for half-and-half. Substitute half-and-half for whipping cream.

Vanilla Pudding Ice Cream

Quick to prepare. Coconut adds interest to the otherwise smooth texture.

2 eggs
1 cup sugar
2 (3-3/4-oz.) pkgs. instant
  vanilla pudding mix

3 cups milk
2 cups half-and-half
1/2 cup flaked coconut

In a large bowl, beat eggs until light and fluffy. Beat in sugar, pudding mix and milk until smooth. Stir in half-and-half and coconut. Pour into ice cream canister. Freeze in ice cream maker according to manufacturer's directions. Makes 2 quarts.

Frozen Custard

Gelatin helps to make this custard extra creamy.

1 cup sugar
1 (.25-oz.) envelope unflavored gelatin
4 cups half-and-half

3 eggs
2 teaspoons vanilla extract
1 cup whipping cream

In a heavy medium saucepan, combine sugar and gelatin. Stir in half-and-half. Stir over medium heat until mixture comes to a boil; set aside. In a small bowl, beat eggs. Gradually stir 1 cup hot gelatin mixture into beaten eggs. Stir egg mixture into remaining gelatin mixture. Stir over low heat until mixture simmers. Cook and stir until mixture thickens slightly, about 1 minute. Stir in vanilla and whipping cream. Cool to room temperature. Pour into ice cream canister. Freeze in ice cream maker according to manufacturer's directions. **Freezer Method:** Pour prepared mixture into a 9-inch square pan or several undivided ice trays. Cover with foil or plastic wrap. Place in freezer; freeze until firm, 3 to 6 hours. Stir 2 or 3 times while freezing. For a smoother texture, freeze prepared mixture until firm; break into small pieces. Spoon half of mixture into a chilled large bowl or chilled food processor bowl. Beat with electric mixer or with metal food processor blade until light and fluffy but not thawed. Repeat with remaining mixture. Serve immediately or return beaten mixture to pan and freeze until firm. Makes about 2 quarts.

Chocolate, Coffee & Tea

Columbus took cocoa beans from America to Europe, but it was Cortez who brought the method for using them. Their use was a closely guarded secret for many years. Today, as you look at the list of flavors in an ice cream store, you'll discover many kinds of chocolate ice cream plus a variety of combinations with other flavors.

Unsweetened chocolate and semisweet chocolate are available in eight-ounce packages which contain eight individually wrapped one-ounce squares. Semisweet chocolate is also available in small teardrop-shaped pieces in six- or twelve-ounce bags. Unsweetened cocoa powder, available in 1/2- to two-pound cans, doesn't require melting and is easy to use.

Chocolate burns easily when placed directly over heat. Melt squares of chocolate in your microwave oven according to oven directions or over hot but not boiling water. Because of its high fat content, melted chocolate solidifies when stirred into a cold mixture. We used this principle in developing Chocolate-Chip Mint Ice Cream. As hot melted semisweet chocolate is stirred into the cold custard-like mixture, bits of chocolate harden, giving a chip effect.

Chocolate and coffee are natural flavor partners. If this combination is one of your weaknesses, you'll want to make Mocha Ice Cream or Toffee-Coffee Ice Cream. If you prefer not to use chocolate, highlight an Irish or Italian dinner party by serving Irish-Coffee Ice Cream or Cappucino Ice Cream.

Tea ice creams and tea ices are very popular in Japanese restaurants. Each is entirely different and enticing. Orange peel, lemon juice and honey introduce a different flavor combination to Citrus Tea Ice. Ginger Tea Ice Cream is rich and smooth with an Oriental flavor emphasized by bits of crystallized ginger. What a way to end an Oriental dinner!

Old-Fashioned Chocolate Ice Cream   *Photo on page 117.*

This is sure to become your favorite chocolate ice cream, just as it is ours.

1-1/3 cups sugar
1 tablespoon cornstarch
1/4 teaspoon salt
3 cups whole milk
2 eggs

3 (1-oz.) squares semisweet chocolate,
  melted
1 (5.33-oz.) can evaporated milk
1 cup whipping cream
1 teaspoon vanilla extract

In a medium saucepan, combine sugar, cornstarch and salt. Stir in whole milk. Stir over medium heat until mixture begins to simmer. In a small bowl, beat eggs. Stir about 1 cup hot milk mixture into beaten eggs. Stir egg mixture into remaining hot milk mixture. Cook and stir over low heat until slightly thickened, about 2 minutes. Stir in melted chocolate. Beat with a whisk until mixture is smooth. Stir in evaporated milk, whipping cream and vanilla. Cool to room temperature. Pour into ice cream canister. Freeze in ice cream maker according to manufacturer's directions. Makes 2 quarts.

Ranch-House Chocolate Ice Cream

An easy-to-make treat for chocolate fans.

1/3 cup unsweetened cocoa powder
1-1/2 cups sugar
1 (13-oz.) can evaporated milk

1 teaspoon vanilla extract
2 cups whipping cream

In a medium saucepan, combine cocoa and sugar. Stir in evaporated milk. Stir over medium heat until cocoa and sugar dissolve; cool to room temperature. Stir in vanilla and whipping cream. Pour into ice cream canister. Freeze in ice cream maker according to manufacturer's directions. Makes about 2 quarts.

Peanut-Butter Fudge Cream

You can't miss with this popular flavor combination.

1 (6-oz.) pkg. semisweet chocolate
  pieces (1 cup)
2 cups milk
1 cup sugar

1/2 cup chunky peanut butter
1 teaspoon vanilla extract
2 cups whipping cream

In a medium saucepan, combine chocolate pieces, milk and sugar. Stir over low heat until chocolate melts. Stir in peanut butter. Cool to room temperature. Stir in vanilla and whipping cream. Pour into ice cream canister. Freeze in ice cream maker according to manufacturer's directions. Makes about 2 quarts.

Rocky Road Ice Cream

Double chocolate flavor appeals to chocaholics.

1/3 cup unsweetened cocoa powder
1 cup sugar
2 cups milk
1 teaspoon vanilla extract
1/8 teaspoon salt

2 cups whipping cream
1 (1-oz.) square semisweet chocolate
1 cup miniature marshmallows
1/2 cup chopped almonds or pecans

In a large saucepan, mix cocoa powder and sugar. Gradually stir in milk. Stir over low heat until sugar and cocoa dissolve. Cool to room temperature. Stir in vanilla, salt and whipping cream; set aside. Shred chocolate with coarse side of grater. Stir shredded chocolate, marshmallows and almonds or pecans into cocoa mixture. Pour into ice cream canister. Freeze in ice cream maker according to manufacturer's directions. Stir marshmallows evenly throughout frozen mixture before serving or ripening. Makes about 2 quarts.

Chocolate-Chip Mint Ice Cream *Photo on page 108.*

Just-right mint flavor with a generous sprinkling of tiny chocolate flecks.

3 eggs
3/4 cup sugar
1 (3-3/4 oz.) pkg. instant
   vanilla pudding mix

1 (13-oz.) can evaporated milk
2 (1-oz.) squares semisweet chocolate
1/2 cup finely chopped buttermints
2 cups half-and-half

In a large bowl, beat eggs until blended. Gradually beat in sugar until thick and lemon colored. Beat in vanilla pudding and evaporated milk until blended. Microwave chocolate until melted or melt over hot water. Stir constantly while slowly pouring hot melted chocolate into egg mixture. Add chopped mints and half-and-half. Pour into ice cream canister. Freeze in ice cream maker according to manufacturer's directions. **Freezer method:** Pour prepared mixture into a 9-inch square pan or several undivided ice trays. Cover with foil or plastic wrap. Place in freezer; freeze until firm, 3 to 6 hours. Stir 2 or 3 times with a fork or spoon while freezing. For a smoother texture, freeze prepared mixture until almost firm, 1 to 3 hours. Break into small pieces. Spoon half of mixture into a chilled large bowl or chilled food processor bowl. Beat with electric mixer or metal food processor blade until light and fluffy but not thawed. Repeat with remaining partially frozen mixture. Serve immediately or return beaten mixture to pan and freeze until firm, 1 to 3 hours. Makes 2 quarts.

Soft Chocolate Ice Cream

Better than commercial soft chocolate ice creams.

1 *teaspoon* unflavored gelatin
2 tablespoons cold water
2 cups whole milk
3/4 cup instant non-fat dry milk powder

1-1/4 cups sugar
1/3 cup unsweetened cocoa powder
2 cups whipping cream
1 teaspoon vanilla extract

In a small saucepan, sprinkle gelatin over cold water to soften. Stir over low heat until gelatin dissolves. Gradually stir in whole milk. In a medium bowl, combine dry milk powder, sugar and cocoa powder. Stir in gelatin mixture. Stir in whipping cream and vanilla. Pour into ice cream canister. Freeze in ice cream maker according to manufacturer's directions. Serve when mixture is firm enough to hold soft peaks but not as firm as regular ice cream. Makes about 2 quarts.

Fudge Ripple Ice Cream

Be sure to make the Fudge Ripple first. Swirl it through any vanilla ice cream.

Fudge Ripple, see below
1 cup sugar
1 tablespoon cornstarch
1/4 teaspoon salt
3 cups whole milk

2 egg yolks
1 (5.33-oz.) can evaporated milk
1 cup whipping cream
1 teaspoon vanilla extract

Fudge Ripple:
1/4 cup sugar
2 tablespoons unsweetened cocoa powder
1/4 cup light corn syrup

2 tablespoons half-and-half
1 tablespoon butter or margarine
1/4 teaspoon vanilla extract

Prepare Fudge Ripple; set aside to cool. In a medium saucepan, combine sugar, cornstarch and salt. Stir in whole milk. Stir over medium heat until mixture begins to simmer. In a small bowl, beat egg yolks. Stir about 1 cup hot milk mixture into beaten egg yolks. Stir egg yolk mixture into remaining hot milk mixture. Cook and stir over low heat until slightly thickened, about 2 minutes. Stir in evaporated milk, whipping cream and vanilla. Cool to room temperature. Pour into ice cream canister. Freeze in ice cream maker according to manufacturer's directions. When frozen, remove lid and dasher from ice cream canister. Insert a long metal spatula into center of ice cream. Pull broad side of spatula toward edge of ice cream canister. Quickly pour cooled Fudge Ripple into space created by moving spatula. Move broad side of spatula back and forth through ice cream and sauce creating a marbled effect. Remove spatula. Cover canister with a double layer of waxed paper. Top with lid. Plug dasher hole with a cork or ball of foil. Ripen in brine, page 12, or place canister in freezer to ripen. Makes 2 quarts.

Fudge Ripple:
In a small saucepan, combine sugar and cocoa powder. Stir in corn syrup and half-and-half. Stir occasionally over medium heat until mixture comes to a boil. Simmer 3 minutes, stirring occasionally. Stir in butter or margarine and vanilla. Set aside to cool.

Chocolate Pudding Ice Cream

Rich and creamy with a strong chocolate flavor.

2 eggs
1 cup sugar
3 cups milk
2 (4-1/2-oz.) pkgs. instant
   chocolate pudding mix

2 cups half-and-half
2 teaspoons vanilla extract

In a large bowl, beat eggs until light and fluffy. Beat in sugar, milk and pudding mix until smooth. Stir in half-and-half and vanilla. Pour into ice cream canister. Freeze in ice cream maker according to manufacturer's directions. Makes 2 quarts.

How to Make Fudge Ripple Ice Cream

1/After ice cream is frozen, remove lid and dasher. Insert metal spatula into center of frozen mixture. Pull to side, creating a hole. Pour in fudge sauce.

2/Move broad side of spatula back and forth through ice cream and sauce creating a marbled effect. Remove spatula. Cover and ripen in brine or in freezer.

Fudge Ice Cream

Dark and super-rich!

6 (1-oz.) squares unsweetened chocolate
2 tablespoons butter or margarine
2 cups sugar
1/3 cup light corn syrup
2/3 cup half-and-half

2 eggs
2 teaspoons vanilla extract
1-1/3 cups half-and-half
2 cups whipping cream

In a heavy medium saucepan, melt chocolate and butter over low heat, stirring often. Stir in sugar, corn syrup and 2/3 cup half-and-half. Stir over medium-low heat until mixture comes to a boil. Simmer 4 minutes without stirring; set aside. In a small bowl, beat eggs until blended. Stir in 1/2 cup hot chocolate mixture. Stir egg mixture into remaining chocolate mixture. Cook and stir over medium heat until slightly thickened, about 1 minute. Cool to lukewarm. Stir in vanilla, 1-1/3 cups half-and-half and whipping cream. Pour into ice cream canister. Freeze in ice cream maker according to manufacturer's directions. Makes about 2 quarts.

Easy Chocolate Sherbet

Typical sherbet texture with a delightful chocolate flavor.

1 (5.5-oz.) can chocolate-flavored syrup
1/2 cup sugar

2-1/2 cups milk
1/2 teaspoon vanilla extract

In a medium bowl, combine chocolate-flavored syrup, sugar, milk and vanilla. Stir until sugar dissolves. Pour into ice cream canister. Freeze in ice cream maker according to manufacturer's directions. Makes about 1 quart.

Mandarin-Chocolate Sherbet

Chocolate with an oriental mystique.

1-1/2 cups sugar
1/2 cup unsweetened cocoa powder
1/4 teaspoon ground cinnamon

4 cups milk
1 cup orange juice
1 teaspoon vanilla extract

In a medium saucepan, combine sugar, cocoa powder and cinnamon. Gradually stir in milk. Cook and stir over low heat until mixture is smooth. Cool to room temperature. Stir in orange juice and vanilla. Pour into ice cream canister. Freeze in ice cream maker according to manufacturer's directions. Makes about 2 quarts.

Toffee-Coffee Ice Cream

Break the wrapped candy bars into coarse or fine pieces by striking with the handle of a knife.

3 eggs, well beaten
2/3 cup sugar
3 cups milk
2 tablespoons instant coffee powder

3 (1-1/16-oz.) toffee candy bars, chilled
1/2 teaspoon vanilla extract
2 cups whipping cream

In a medium saucepan, combine beaten eggs, sugar, milk and coffee powder. Cook and stir over low heat until sugar and coffee powder dissolve and mixture thickens slightly. Cool to room temperature. Break chilled candy in wrappers into coarse or fine pieces by striking sharply with handle of a knife. Stir broken candy, vanilla and whipping cream into cooled mixture. Pour into ice cream canister. Freeze in ice cream maker according to manufacturer's directions. Makes 2 quarts.

Irish-Coffee Ice Cream

Make this as a surprise treat on St. Patrick's Day.

2 eggs, well beaten
2 cups milk
1 cup firmly packed brown sugar
4 tablespoons instant coffee powder

1/2 cup Irish whiskey or brandy
2 teaspoons vanilla extract
2 cups whipping cream

In a medium saucepan, combine beaten eggs, milk, brown sugar and instant coffee. Cook and stir over medium-low heat until sugar and coffee dissolve and mixture thickens slightly. Remove from heat; stir in whiskey or brandy. Cool to room temperature. Stir in vanilla and whipping cream. Pour into ice cream canister. Freeze in ice cream maker according to manufacturer's directions. Makes 2 quarts.

Cappucino Ice Cream

Strong-coffee fans will ask for seconds of this delightful dessert.

1/2 teaspoon ground cinnamon
2 cups sugar
6 tablespoons instant coffee powder
2 tablespoons unsweetened cocoa powder

1-1/2 cups boiling water
2 cups half-and-half
2 cups whipping cream
1/4 cup brandy or cognac

In a large bowl, combine cinnamon, sugar, coffee powder and cocoa powder. Stir in boiling water until sugar dissolves. Cool to room temperature. Stir in half-and-half and whipping cream. Stir in brandy or cognac. Pour into ice cream canister. Freeze in ice cream maker according to manufacturer's directions. Makes about 2 quarts.

Mocha Ice Cream

A good strong coffee flavor with a chocolate base.

1/2 cup unsweetened cocoa powder
2 tablespoons instant coffee powder
3/4 cup sugar
1/2 cup milk

1 teaspoon vanilla extract
4 cups half-and-half
1 cup whipping cream

In a small saucepan, combine cocoa powder, coffee powder and sugar. Gradually stir in milk. Stir over medium heat until mixture begins to boil. Cool to room temperature. In a large bowl, combine cocoa mixture, vanilla, half-and-half and whipping cream. Pour into ice cream canister. Freeze in ice cream maker according to manufacturer's directions. Makes about 2 quarts.

Café au Lait Ice Cream

Simple to make and elegant to serve!

2 egg yolks, beaten
2/3 cup sugar
1 cup milk
2 tablespoon instant coffee powder

1/4 cup miniature marshmallows
1/2 teaspoon vanilla extract
2 egg whites
1 cup whipping cream

In a medium saucepan, combine beaten egg yolks, sugar and milk. Cook and stir over low heat until mixture thickens and coats a metal spoon. Stir in coffee powder. Stir in marshmallows until melted. Stir in vanilla. Set aside to cool 15 minutes. In a small bowl, beat egg whites until stiff but not dry. Fold into egg yolk mixture. In a medium bowl, whip cream until soft peaks form. Fold into egg yolk mixture. Pour into a 9'' x 5'' loaf pan or several undivided ice trays. Cover with foil or plastic wrap. Place in freezer; freeze until firm, 3 to 6 hours. Stir 2 or 3 times with a fork or spoon while freezing. Makes about 1 quart.

Mexican Mocha Créme

Rich robust combination of chocolate, coffee and Kahlua.

1 cup half-and-half
2 teaspoons instant coffee powder
3 (1-oz.) squares semisweet chocolate
4 egg yolks

2/3 cup sugar
1 tablespoon butter
1 cup whipping cream
2 tablespoons Kahlua

In a medium saucepan, combine half-and-half and coffee powder. Cut chocolate into small chunks; add to coffee mixture. Stir over low heat until chocolate melts; set aside. In a large bowl, beat egg yolks and sugar until thick and lemon colored. Stir 1/2 cup hot chocolate mixture into beaten egg yolk mixture. Stir egg yolk mixture into remaining chocolate mixture. Cook and stir over low heat until mixture thickens, about 5 minutes. Stir in butter. Cool on a rack 10 to 15 minutes. Stir in whipping cream and Kahlua. Pour into ice cream canister. Freeze in ice cream maker according to manufacturer's directions. Makes about 1 quart.

How to Make Café au Lait Ice Cream

1/After egg-and-milk mixture thickens, add marshmallows and coffee powder. Remove from heat; stir until marshmallows melt.

2/Freeze until firm, 3 to 6 hours. To break up ice crystals, stir 2 or 3 times as mixture freezes. This makes a smooth ice cream.

Citrus Tea Ice

Refreshing treat for a hot Summer's eve.

6 cups water
1 cup honey
2 teaspoons grated orange peel

6 tea bags
1/4 cup lemon juice

In a large saucepan, combine water, honey and orange peel. Stir over medium heat until mixture comes to a boil; remove from heat. Add tea bags. Cover and steep 5 minutes. Remove tea bags; cool syrup to room temperature. Stir in lemon juice. Pour into ice cream canister. Freeze in ice cream maker according to manufacturer's directions. **Freezer method:** Pour prepared mixture into a 9-inch square pan or several undivided ice trays. Cover with foil or plastic wrap. Place in freezer; freeze until firm, 3 to 6 hours. Scrape frozen mixture with a fork until pieces resemble finely crushed ice. For a smoother texture, freeze prepared mixture until firm; break into small pieces. Spoon half of mixture into chilled food processor bowl. Beat with metal blade until smooth and fluffy but not thawed. Repeat with remaining mixture. Serve immediately or return beaten mixture to pan and freeze until firm, 1 to 3 hours. Makes about 2 quarts.

Minted Tea Ice

Beating this in a food processor gives it a light and fluffy texture.

3 cups water
1/4 cup light corn syrup

1/2 cup butter mints
3 tea bags

In a medium saucepan, combine water, corn syrup and butter mints. Stir occasionally over medium heat until mixture comes to a boil and mints dissolve. Remove from heat; add tea bags. Cover and let steep about 5 minutes. Remove and discard tea bags; cool syrup to room temperature. Pour prepared mixture into a 9" x 5" loaf pan or several undivided ice trays. Cover with foil or plastic wrap. Place in freezer; freeze until firm, 3 to 6 hours. Scrape frozen mixture with a fork until pieces resemble finely crushed ice. For a smoother texture, freeze prepared mixture until firm; break into small pieces. Spoon into chilled food processor bowl. Beat with metal blade until light and fluffy but not thawed. Serve immediately or return beaten mixture to pan and freeze until firm, 1 to 3 hours. Makes 6 servings.

Ginger Tea Ice Cream

Unbelievably smooth and impressive.

8 egg yolks
1 cup sugar
4 cups whipping cream

2 tablespoons instant tea powder
1/4 cup finely chopped crystallized ginger

In a large bowl, beat egg yolks and sugar until well blended. Stir in whipping cream, tea powder and ginger. Pour into a large saucepan. Cook and stir over low heat until slightly thickened. Cool to room temperature. Pour into ice cream canister. Freeze in ice cream maker according to manufacturer's directions. Makes about 2 quarts.

Fruits of the Vine

Do you recall the grape, strawberry and raspberry flavored snow cones of your childhood? These fruits of the vine are still some of the most requested ice cream and sherbet flavors. With these recipes you can prepare homemade fresh blueberry, boysenberry, raspberry or strawberry ice cream for a back yard barbecue or picnic. Mix the ingredients in your kitchen, then freeze in the freezer or pour into an ice cream maker. Place the ice cream maker on the back porch or under a shade tree before layering ice and salt around the filled canister in the bucket. Freeze it right there and serve it immediately. For a picnic, freeze it at home, then follow instructions for ripening ice cream on page 12. Serve it directly from the canister.

When you're making ice cream with berries, there's always the question of whether or not to remove the seeds. We tried both ways and have indicated our preference in each recipe. Strawberry seeds are not usually objectionable, but it's unpleasant to bite down on frozen raspberry or boysenberry seeds. When fresh berries are not in season, use some of the recipes which call for frozen berries.

Although not usually considered for homemade ice creams, we included grapes because they are fruits of the vine. Try Grape Punch Sorbet for a refreshing surprise at your next committee meeting or Girl Scout get-together. Serve it frozen like a sorbet in a dessert dish or spoon the partially frozen mixture into wine glasses and serve while it's still icy.

Buy packages of fresh cranberries when they are available and keep them in your freezer for year-round use. You'll be proud to serve light and refreshing Cranberry-Wine Sorbet after an important dinner any time of the year.

Old-Fashioned Strawberry Ice Cream   *Photo on cover.*

Rich and creamy even when you substitute half-and-half for the whipping cream.

3 cups fresh strawberries
2 eggs
1-1/4 cups sugar

2 cups half-and-half
1/4 teaspoon vanilla extract
1 cup whipping cream

Wash strawberries; remove and discard caps. Puree berries in blender or food processor; set aside. In a large bowl, beat eggs until thick and lemon colored. Beat in sugar, half-and-half, vanilla and whipping cream. Stir in blended strawberries. Pour into ice cream canister. Freeze in ice cream maker according to manufacturer's directions. Makes about 2 quarts.

Strawberry Cream

So rich and creamy it doesn't have to be stirred or beaten while freezing.

3 cups fresh strawberries
3 egg yolks
1-1/2 cups sugar

1-1/2 cups whipping cream
3 egg whites

Wash strawberries; remove and discard caps. Puree berries in blender or food processor. Pour into a strainer over a medium bowl. Press puree through strainer with back of a spoon; set aside. Discard seeds. In a large bowl, beat egg yolks until thick and lemon colored. Beat in sugar and whipping cream until soft peaks form. Stir in strained berries; set aside. In a medium bowl, beat egg whites until stiff but not dry. Fold into berry mixture. Pour into a 9-inch square pan. Cover with foil or plastic wrap. Place in freezer; freeze until firm, 3 to 6 hours. Makes about 2 quarts.

Pronto Strawberry Cream

It's easy to make this smooth ice cream in an ice cream maker or freezer.

1 pt. fresh strawberries
1/2 cup sugar
1 tablespoon lemon juice

1 (14-oz.) can sweetened condensed milk
1 cup whole milk
2 to 4 drops red food coloring, if desired

Wash strawberries; remove and discard caps. Puree berries in blender or food processor until almost smooth. In a large bowl, combine pureed berries, sugar, lemon juice, sweetened condensed milk, whole milk and food coloring, if desired. Pour into ice cream canister. Freeze in ice cream maker according to manufacturer's directions. **Freezer method:** Pour prepared mixture into a 9" x 5" loaf pan or several undivided ice trays. Cover with foil or plastic wrap. Place in freezer; freeze until firm, 3 to 6 hours. Stir 2 or 3 times with a fork or spoon while freezing. For a smoother texture, freeze prepared mixture until almost firm, 1 to 3 hours, then break into small pieces. Spoon into a chilled large bowl or chilled food processor bowl. Beat with electric mixer or metal food processor blade until light and fluffy but not thawed. Serve immediately or return beaten mixture to pan and freeze until firm, 1 to 3 hours. Makes about 1 quart.

Strawberry Italian Cream

Strawberry lovers delight with an Italian flair!

1 qt. fresh strawberries
1-1/2 cups sugar
2 tablespoons light corn syrup

2/3 cup water
2 egg whites
1 cup whipping cream

Wash strawberries; remove and discard caps. Puree berries in blender or food processor; set aside. In a medium saucepan, combine sugar, corn syrup and water. Stir over medium heat until sugar dissolves. Stirring occasionally, cook to 234°F (112°C) on a candy thermometer or until syrup spins a 2-inch thread when slowly poured from a spoon; set aside. In a medium bowl, beat egg whites until stiff but not dry. Beating constantly, immediately pour in hot syrup in a thin stream. Continue beating until cool and thick. Stir in pureed berries; set aside. In a medium bowl, whip cream until soft peaks form. Fold into berry mixture. Spoon into a 9-inch square pan or several undivided ice trays. Cover with foil or plastic wrap. Place in freezer; freeze until firm, 3 to 6 hours. Makes about 2 quarts.

Frozen Strawberry Yogurt

Good and good for you!

1 pt. fresh strawberries
2 cups plain yogurt

3/4 cup sugar
1/2 teaspoon vanilla extract

Wash strawberries; remove and discard caps. Puree berries in blender or food processor until almost smooth; set aside. In a medium bowl, stir yogurt until smooth. Stir in sugar and vanilla. Stir in pureed berries until well blended. Pour into ice cream canister. Freeze in ice cream maker according to manufacturer's directions. Makes about 5 cups.

Creamy Strawberry Yogurt

Heavenly strawberry color with a slightly tart yogurt taste.

1 (3-oz.) pkg. strawberry-flavored gelatin
3/4 cup sugar
1 cup water

1 pt. fresh strawberries
2 cups plain yogurt
1 cup whipping cream

In a medium saucepan, combine gelatin and sugar. Stir in water. Stir over medium heat until gelatin dissolves; set aside. Wash strawberries; remove and discard caps. Puree berries in blender or food processor. Stir into gelatin mixture; set aside. In a medium bowl, stir yogurt. Stir in strawberry mixture and whipping cream. Pour into ice cream canister. Freeze in ice cream maker according to manufacturer's directions. Makes about 2 quarts.

Frozen Strawberry Sour Cream

This velvet smooth pink creation will freeze rapidly if you use lots of salt and ice.

1 pt. fresh strawberries	**1 cup dairy sour cream**
3 eggs	**1 cup whipping cream**
1 cup sugar	**1/2 teaspoon vanilla extract**

Wash strawberries; remove and discard caps. Puree berries in blender or food processor; set aside. In a large bowl, beat eggs and sugar until thick and creamy, 4 to 5 minutes. Stir in pureed berries, sour cream, whipping cream and vanilla. Pour into ice cream canister. Freeze in ice cream maker according to manufacturer's directions. Makes about 2 quarts.

Strawberry Sherbet

Gelatin reduces the formation of ice crystals when you store this in your freezer.

1 *teaspoon* unflavored gelatin	**1-1/2 cups sugar**
2 tablespoons lemon juice	**1 qt. fresh strawberries**
2 cups milk	

In a small bowl, sprinkle gelatin over lemon juice; set aside. In a medium saucepan, combine milk and sugar. Stir over low heat until sugar dissolves. Stir in softened gelatin; set aside. Wash strawberries; remove and discard caps. Puree berries in blender or food processor. Stir into milk mixture. Cool to room temperature. Pour into ice cream canister. Freeze in ice cream maker according to manufacturer's directions. **Freezer method:** Pour prepared mixture into a 9-inch square pan or several undivided ice trays. Cover with foil or plastic wrap. Place in freezer; freeze until firm, 3 to 6 hours. For a smoother texture, freeze prepared mixture until firm; break into small pieces. Spoon half of mixture into a chilled large bowl or chilled food processor bowl. Beat with electric mixer or metal food processor blade until light and fluffy. Repeat with remaining frozen mixture. Serve immediately or return beaten mixture to pan and freeze until firm, 1 to 3 hours. Makes about 2 quarts.

*Stir yogurt and sour cream before adding
them to an ice cream mixture.*

Strawberry Ice

A superb strawberry flavor with a light texture.

1 *teaspoon* unflavored gelatin	2 cups water
2 tablespoons lemon juice	1 qt. fresh strawberries
1-1/2 cups sugar	

In a small bowl, sprinkle gelatin over lemon juice; set aside. In a medium saucepan, combine sugar and water. Stir over medium heat until sugar dissolves and mixture comes to a boil. Stir in softened gelatin. Wash strawberries; remove and discard caps. Puree berries in blender or food processor. Stir pureed berries into syrup mixture. Cool to room temperature. Pour into ice cream canister. Freeze in ice cream maker according to manufacturer's directions. **Freezer method:** Pour prepared mixture into a 9-inch square pan or several undivided ice trays. Cover with foil or plastic wrap. Place in freezer; freeze until firm, 3 to 6 hours. Scrape frozen mixture with a fork until pieces resemble finely crushed ice. Serve immediately. For a smoother texture, freeze prepared mixture until firm; break into small pieces. Spoon half of mixture into chilled food processor bowl. Beat with metal blade until light and fluffy but not thawed. Repeat with remaining frozen mixture. Serve immediately or return beaten mixture to pan and freeze until firm, 1 to 3 hours. Makes about 2 quarts.

Strawberry-Rhubarb Sorbet

Who can resist this flavor combination?

1 lb. fresh rhubarb,	1-1/2 cups sugar
cut in 1-inch pieces (4 cups)	1 pt. fresh strawberries
1/4 cup water	

In a medium saucepan, combine rhubarb and water. Bring to a boil over medium heat. Cover and simmer until rhubarb is tender, about 5 minutes. Stir in sugar until dissolved. Puree rhubarb mixture in blender or food processor until smooth. Pour into a large bowl; set aside. Wash strawberries. Remove and discard caps. Process in blender or food processor until almost smooth. Stir into rhubarb mixture. Pour into a 9'' x 5'' loaf pan or several undivided ice trays. Cover with foil or plastic wrap. Place in freezer; freeze until firm, 3 to 6 hours. Scrape frozen mixture with a fork until pieces resemble finely crushed ice. Serve immediately. For a smoother texture, freeze prepared mixture until firm; break into small pieces. Spoon into chilled food processor bowl. Beat with metal blade until light and fluffy but not thawed. Serve immediately or return beaten mixture to pan and freeze until firm, 1 to 3 hours. Makes about 5 cups.

Strawberries keep better and longer if they are washed and capped just before making ice cream.

Frozen Strawberry Wine

When frozen, this mixture should be soft but not slushy.

1 cup fresh strawberries
3/4 cup light corn syrup

2 cups dry white wine
2 or 3 drops red food coloring, if desired

Wash strawberries. Remove and discard caps. Process berries in blender or food processor until almost smooth. In a medium bowl, combine pureed berries, corn syrup, wine and food coloring, if desired. Pour into ice cream canister. Freeze in ice cream maker according to manufacturer's directions. **Freezer method:** Pour prepared mixture into a 9'' x 5'' loaf pan or several undivided ice trays. Cover with foil or plastic wrap. Place in freezer; freeze until almost firm, 1 to 3 hours. Scrape frozen mixture with a fork until pieces resemble finely crushed ice. Serve immediately. For a smoother texture, freeze prepared mixture until firm, break into small pieces. Spoon into chilled food processor bowl. Beat with metal blade until light and fluffy but not thawed. Mixture will be soft but not slushy. Spoon into wine glasses; serve immediately with a spoon. Suggest guests drink the mixture as it melts. Makes 1 quart.

Strawberry Sorbet

Use thoroughly ripe strawberries for the best flavor.

1 cup water
3/4 cup sugar

1 pt. fresh strawberries
1/2 cup orange juice

In a small saucepan, combine water and sugar. Stir over low heat until sugar dissolves; bring to a boil. Boil gently 5 minutes without stirring; set aside to cool. Wash strawberries; remove and discard caps. Puree strawberries in blender or food processor until almost smooth. In a medium bowl, combine pureed strawberries, cooled syrup and orange juice. Pour into a 9'' x 5'' loaf pan or several undivided ice trays. Cover with foil or plastic wrap. Place in freezer; freeze until almost firm, 1 to 3 hours. Stir 2 or 3 times with a fork or spoon while freezing. For a smoother texture, freeze prepared mixture until almost firm; break into small pieces. Spoon into chilled food processor bowl. Beat with metal blade until light and fluffy but not thawed. Serve immediately or return beaten mixture to pan and freeze until firm, 1 to 3 hours. Makes about 1 quart.

Cranberry-Wine Sorbet

Smelling the wonderful aroma of cranberries cooking in wine is almost as great as eating the sorbet.

2 cups fresh or frozen whole cranberries
1/2 cup burgundy wine
1-1/2 cups orange juice

1 cup sugar
1 teaspoon grated orange peel

In a medium saucepan, combine all ingredients. Stir over medium heat until cranberries are soft and break open. Pour into a fine strainer over a medium bowl. Press as much juice and pulp as possible through strainer with back of a spoon; discard remaining pulp. Cool strained puree to room temperature. Pour into ice cream canister. Freeze in ice cream maker according to manufacturer's directions. **Freezer method:** Pour prepared mixture into a 9" x 5" loaf pan or several undivided ice trays. Cover with foil or plastic wrap. Place in freezer; freeze until firm, 3 to 6 hours. Scrape frozen mixture with a fork until pieces resemble finely crushed ice. For a smoother texture, freeze prepared mixture until firm; break into small pieces. Spoon into chilled food processor bowl. Beat with metal blade until light and fluffy but not thawed. Serve immediately or return beaten mixture to pan and freeze until firm, 1 to 3 hours. Makes about 3 cups.

Cranberry-Orange Ice

Refreshing as a cool summer breeze.

2 cups sugar
2 cups orange juice

4 cups cranberry juice cocktail

In a medium saucepan, combine sugar and orange juice. Stir over medium heat until sugar dissolves. Cool to room temperature. Stir in cranberry juice cocktail. Pour into ice cream canister. Freeze in ice cream maker according to manufacturer's directions. **Freezer method:** Pour prepared mixture into a 9-inch square pan or several undivided ice trays. Cover with foil or plastic wrap. Place in freezer; freeze until firm, 3 to 6 hours. Scrape frozen mixture with a fork until pieces resemble finely crushed ice. Serve immediately. For a smoother texture, freeze prepared mixture until firm; break into small pieces. Spoon half of mixture into chilled food processor bowl. Beat with metal blade until smooth and fluffy but not thawed. Repeat with remaining frozen mixture. Serve immediately or return beaten mixture to pan and freeze until firm, 1 to 3 hours. Makes about 2 quarts.

1/Heat cranberries in wine mixture until cranberries are soft and break open. Mixture will be slightly foamy on top.

2/When cranberry mixture is solid, make an attractive arrangement in a dessert dish by scooping with a miniature ice cream scoop.

How to Make Cranberry-Wine Sorbet

Orange-Cranberry Sherbet

Especially pleasing at the end of a large holiday meal.

2 cups sugar
1 (.25-oz.) envelope unflavored gelatin
2 teaspoons grated orange peel

3 cups milk
2 cups fresh or frozen whole cranberries
1 cup orange juice

In a medium saucepan, combine sugar, gelatin and orange peel. Stir in milk. Stir over low heat until sugar and gelatin dissolve; set aside. In blender or food processor puree cranberries and orange juice until almost smooth. Stir into milk mixture until blended. Pour into ice cream canister. Freeze in ice cream maker according to manufacturer's directions. Makes about 2 quarts.

Raspberry Ice Cream

For a tasty surprise, pour a little Crème de Cassis over each serving.

2 (10-oz.) pkgs. frozen raspberries, thawed	**1 cup sugar**
4 eggs	**2 teaspoons lemon juice**
	2 cups half-and-half

Puree thawed raspberries in blender or food processor. Pour into a fine strainer. Use back of a spoon to press puree through strainer into a large bowl; discard seeds. Set puree aside. Beat eggs and sugar in blender or food processor until smooth. Stir egg mixture, lemon juice and half-and-half into raspberry puree until blended. Pour into ice cream canister. Freeze in ice cream maker according to manufacturer's directions. Makes about 2 quarts.

Raspberry-Melon Sorbet

Summer-sweet melon makes this frosty and refreshing.

1 (10-oz.) pkg. frozen raspberries, thawed	**1 large ripe honeydew melon, peeled**
	1/4 cup sugar

Puree raspberries in blender or food processor. Pour into a fine strainer. Use back of a spoon to press puree through strainer into a medium bowl; set aside. Discard seeds. Remove melon seeds. Cut fruit into cubes. Puree half at a time in blender or food processor. Pour melon puree into strained raspberry puree. Add sugar; stir to blend. Pour into ice cream canister. Freeze in ice cream maker according to manufacturer's directions. **Freezer method:** Pour prepared mixture into a 9-inch square pan or several undivided ice trays. Cover with foil or plastic wrap. Place in freezer; freeze until firm, 3 to 6 hours. Scrape frozen mixture with a fork until pieces resemble finely crushed ice. For a smoother texture, freeze prepared mixture until firm; break into small pieces. Spoon half of mixture into chilled food processor bowl. Beat with metal blade until light and fluffy but not thawed. Repeat with remaining frozen mixture. Serve immediately or return beaten mixture to pan and freeze until firm, 1 to 3 hours. Makes 2 quarts.

Raspberry Yogurt Creme

Raspberry flavor with a tang.

1 (10-oz.) pkg. frozen raspberries, partially thawed	**1 (7-oz.) jar marshmallow creme**
	2 cups plain yogurt

Puree raspberries in blender or food processor. Pour into a fine strainer. Use back of a spoon to press puree through strainer into a small bowl; discard seeds. Pour strained berries into blender or food processor. Add marshmallow; blend until smooth. In a large bowl, stir yogurt until smooth. Gradually stir in berry mixture. Pour into ice cream canister. Freeze in ice cream maker according to manufacturer's directions. **Freezer method:** Pour prepared mixture into a 9'' x 5'' loaf pan or several undivided ice trays. Cover with foil or plastic wrap. Place in freezer; freeze until firm, 3 to 6 hours. Stir with a spoon or fork 2 or 3 times while freezing. Makes 1 quart.

Fresh Raspberry Ice Cream

Nothing else can compare with fresh raspberry flavor.

4 cups fresh raspberries (2 baskets)
2 eggs
1-1/3 cups sugar
1/4 cup light corn syrup

1 cup whipping cream
1-1/2 cups half-and-half
1 tablespoon lemon juice

Wash raspberries; puree in blender or food processor until almost smooth. Pour into a fine strainer. Use the back of a spoon to press puree through strainer into a small bowl; discard seeds. Set puree aside. In a medium bowl, beat eggs and sugar until thick and lemon colored, 4 to 5 minutes. Stir in raspberry puree, corn syrup, whipping cream, half-and-half and lemon juice. Pour into ice cream canister. Freeze in ice cream maker according to manufacturer's directions. **Freezer method:** Pour prepared mixture into a 9-inch square pan or several undivided ice trays. Cover with foil or plastic wrap. Place in freezer; freeze until firm, 3 to 6 hours. Stir 2 or 3 times with a fork or spoon while freezing. For a smoother texture, freeze prepared mixture until almost firm, 1 to 3 hours; break into small pieces. Spoon half of mixture into a chilled large bowl or chilled food processor bowl. Beat with electric mixer or metal food processor blade until light and fluffy but not thawed. Repeat with remaining mixture. Serve immediately or return beaten mixture to pan and freeze until firm, 1 to 3 hours. Makes about 2 quarts.

Framboise Sherbet

Superb flavor combination popular in France.

2 (10-oz.) pkgs. frozen raspberries,
  thawed
3/4 cup currant jelly

1/4 cup Crème de Cassis
2 cups half-and-half

Press thawed raspberries through a fine strainer into a small saucepan; discard seeds. Add currant jelly to raspberry puree. Stir over low heat until jelly dissolves. Cool to lukewarm. Stir in liqueur and half-and-half. Pour into a 9'' x 5'' loaf pan or several undivided ice trays. Cover with foil or plastic wrap. Place in freezer; freeze until almost firm, 1 to 3 hours. Break into small pieces. Spoon into a chilled large bowl or chilled food processor bowl. Beat with electric mixer or metal food processor blade until smooth and fluffy but not thawed. Serve immediately or return beaten mixture to pan and freeze until firm, 1 to 3 hours. Makes about 1 quart.

If you don't have a blender or food processor, mash berries with your electric mixer or a potato masher.

1/When partially frozen, use a spoon to break the mixture into chunks. Beat sherbet pieces in electric mixer until fluffy but not thawed.

2/Beat egg whites until stiff but not dry. Fold beaten egg whites into beaten frozen mixture. Return to freezer and freeze until firm.

How to Make Grape Sherbet

Grape Slush

Reminiscent of old-fashioned snow cones when served immediately after freezing.

2 cups grape juice
1 cup cold water

1/3 cup light corn syrup

In a medium bowl, combine grape juice and water. Stir in corn syrup. Pour into ice cream canister. Freeze in ice cream maker according to manufacturer's directions. **Freezer method:** Pour prepared mixture into a 9'' x 5'' loaf pan or several undivided ice trays. Cover with foil or plastic wrap. Place in freezer; freeze until firm, 3 to 6 hours. Scrape frozen mixture with a fork until pieces resemble finely crushed ice. Serve immediately. For a smoother texture, freeze prepared mixture until firm; break into small pieces. Spoon into chilled food processor bowl. Beat with metal blade until smooth and fluffy but not thawed. Serve immediately or return beaten mixture to pan and freeze until firm, 1 to 3 hours. Makes 1 quart.

Grape Sherbet

The freezer method variation using beaten egg whites gives a smoother, more fluffy texture.

1 cup water
2/3 cup sugar
2/3 cup light corn syrup

1 teaspoon grated lemon peel
4 cups grape juice
1/2 cup lemon juice

In a medium saucepan, combine water, sugar, corn syrup and lemon peel. Stir over medium heat until sugar dissolves. Cool to room temperature. Stir in grape juice and lemon juice. Pour into canister. Freeze in ice cream maker according to manufacturer's directions. **Freezer method:** Pour prepared mixture into a 9-inch square pan or several undivided ice trays. Cover with foil or plastic wrap. Place in freezer; freeze until firm, 3 to 6 hours. Stir 2 or 3 times with a fork or spoon while freezing. Makes about 2 quarts.

Variation

For a smoother texture, freeze mixture until almost firm, 1 to 3 hours. In a large bowl, beat 4 egg whites until stiff but not dry; set aside. Break partially frozen mixture into small pieces. Spoon into a large chilled bowl. Beat with electric mixer until smooth but not thawed. Fold in beaten egg whites. Spoon into a 2-quart container. Cover with foil or plastic wrap. Place in freezer; freeze until firm, 1 to 3 hours.

Grape Punch Sorbet

Reminds you of traditional fruit punch.

1/3 cup sugar
1/3 cup light corn syrup
2 cups grape juice
2 (6-oz.) cans pineapple juice
**   (1-1/2 cups)**

1 cup orange juice
1 (12-oz.) can lemon-lime soda

In a medium saucepan, combine sugar, corn syrup and grape juice. Stir over medium heat until sugar dissolves. Stir in pineapple juice, orange juice and lemon-lime soda. Cool to room temperature. Pour into ice cream canister. Freeze in ice cream maker according to manufacturer's directions. If frozen mixture has a two-tone grape color, stir with a spoon or fork before serving or storing. Makes about 2 quarts.

Blueberry-Orange Yogurt

You won't need to stir this to get a smooth and creamy texture.

1 cup fresh or frozen blueberries
3/4 cup sugar
1/4 cup water
2 egg whites

1/8 teaspoon cream of tartar
2 cups mandarin orange flavored yogurt
1/8 teaspoon almond extract

Puree blueberries in blender or food processor. Pour into a fine strainer over a small bowl. Press puree through strainer with back of a spoon to remove seeds and bits of peel; set aside. Discard seeds and peel. In a small saucepan, combine sugar and water. Bring to a boil; stir until sugar dissolves. Boil without stirring until syrup reaches 238°F (114°C) on a candy thermometer or syrup forms a soft ball when dropped into very cold water, 10 to 15 minutes. In a medium bowl, beat egg whites and cream of tartar until soft peaks form. Beating constantly, immediately pour hot syrup in a thin stream over beaten egg whites. Continue beating until cool and thick; set aside. In a large bowl, stir yogurt until smooth. Stir in almond extract and pureed blueberries. Gradually fold in egg white mixture. Spoon into a 9" x 5" loaf pan or several undivided ice trays. Cover with foil or plastic wrap. Place in freezer; freeze until firm, 3 to 6 hours. Makes about 4-1/2 cups.

Blueberry Sorbet

For a smooth texture, strain the mixture to remove tiny pieces of peel and seeds.

1 cup sugar
1/2 cup light corn syrup
1 cup water

1 qt. fresh blueberries
1/4 cup lemon juice

In a small saucepan, combine sugar, corn syrup and water. Stir over low heat until sugar dissolves; set aside. Wash blueberries. Puree in blender or food processor. Strain, if desired. In a medium bowl, combine pureed blueberries, lemon juice and syrup. Cool to room temperature. Pour into ice cream canister. Freeze in ice cream maker according to manufacturer's directions. **Freezer method:** Pour prepared mixture into a 9" x 5" loaf pan or several undivided ice trays. Cover with foil or plastic wrap. Place in freezer; freeze until firm, 3 to 6 hours. Stir with a fork or spoon 2 or 3 times while freezing. Break frozen mixture into pieces. Spoon into chilled food processor bowl. Beat with metal blade until light and fluffy but not thawed. Serve immediately or return beaten mixture to pan and freeze until firm, 1 to 3 hours. Makes about 6 cups.

If cooked mixtures appear to curdle, they will become smooth when churned in your ice cream maker.

Boysenberry Ice Cream

Frozen boysenberries are available in supermarkets throughout the year.

**1 (20-oz.) pkg. frozen whole
   unsweetened boysenberries, thawed**
2 cups whipping cream

1 cup half-and-half
1 cup sugar
2 eggs, well beaten

Puree thawed boysenberries in blender or food processor. Pour into a fine strainer over a large bowl. Press puree through strainer with back of a spoon to remove seeds; discard seeds. Stir in whipping cream, half-and-half, sugar and beaten eggs until sugar dissolves. Pour into canister. Freeze in ice cream maker according to manufacturer's directions. **Freezer method:** Pour prepared mixture into a 9-inch square pan or several undivided ice trays. Cover with foil or plastic wrap. Place in freezer; freeze until firm, 3 to 6 hours. Stir 2 or 3 times with a fork or spoon while freezing. For a smoother texture, freeze prepared mixture until almost firm, 1 to 3 hours; break into small pieces. Spoon half of partially frozen mixture into a large chilled bowl or chilled food processor bowl. Beat with electric mixer or metal food processor blade until light and fluffy but not thawed. Repeat with remaining partially frozen mixture. Serve immediately or return beaten mixture to pan and freeze until firm, 1 to 3 hours. Makes about 2 quarts.

How to Tell When a Mixture Coats a Spoon

To tell when a custard mixture coats a metal spoon, dip it into the mixture. Pull your finger across the center back of the spoon. If the mixture doesn't run into the line left by your finger, the mixture has cooked long enough.

Citrus Fruits

Everybody loves homemade ice cream. The flavor you make depends on what you like plus the availability of ingredients. That's where citrus fruits have the advantage over other fruits. They are in every market every day of the year.

Fortunately, lemons know no season. On the same tree, there are buds, blossoms, small unripened lemons and ready-to-pick fruit. As the fruit matures, it is picked and shipped to markets throughout the world. Meanwhile, fruit left on the tree is going through the ripening process.

Make an impressive dessert by cutting three or four oranges in half. Juice the oranges being careful not to damage the peeling, or scoop the pulp out and use it in the recipe. Use the orange peel halves, fresh or frozen, as bowls.

Although we think there's nothing else to compare with freshly squeezed orange juice, these citrus recipes are excellent when made with reconstituted frozen orange juice or orange juice from cartons found in dairy cases. Do not substitute orange drinks, carbonated orange-flavored soda or orangeade in any of the recipes. The result will not be the same.

Although limes have a beautiful green color, the juice is not much darker than lemon juice. Add several drops of green food coloring to lime recipes to be frozen in the freezer. If the mixture will be churned in an ice cream maker, add enough food coloring to make an *intense* color. As the ice cream churns, volume increases and color diminishes. Food coloring does not change the flavor or texture, only the color.

Orange-Pineapple Sherbet

Sour cream gives this traditional flavor combination a very smooth texture.

3/4 cup light corn syrup
2 cups dairy sour cream
1 (8-oz.) can crushed pineapple with
  juice

1 (6-oz.) can frozen orange juice
  concentrate, thawed

In a medium bowl, stir corn syrup into sour cream, until smooth. Stir in pineapple with juice and undiluted orange juice concentrate. Pour into ice cream canister. Freeze in ice cream maker according to manufacturer's directions. **Freezer method:** Pour mixture into a 9" x 5" loaf pan or several undivided ice trays. Cover with foil or plastic wrap. Place in freezer; freeze until firm, 3 to 6 hours. Stir 2 or 3 times while freezing. For a smoother texture, break frozen mixture into small pieces. Spoon half of mixture into a large chilled bowl or chilled food processor bowl. Beat with electric mixer or metal food processor blade until light and fluffy but not thawed. Repeat with remaining frozen mixture. Return to pan and freeze until firm, 1 to 3 hours. Makes about 6 cups.

Orange-Honey Yogurt   *Photo on page 108.*

For those who like the taste of honey.

2 cups plain yogurt
1 (6-oz.) can frozen orange juice
  concentrate, partially thawed

1/2 cup honey
1/2 cup half-and-half

In a medium bowl, stir yogurt until smooth. Stir in undiluted orange juice concentrate, honey and half-and-half. Pour into a 9" x 5" loaf pan or several undivided ice trays. Cover with foil or plastic wrap. Place in freezer; freeze until almost firm, 1 to 3 hours. Stir 2 or 3 times while freezing. For a smoother texture, break frozen mixture into small pieces. Spoon into a large chilled bowl or chilled food processor bowl. Beat with electric mixer or metal food processor blade until smooth and fluffy but not thawed. Return to pan and freeze until firm, 1 to 3 hours. Makes about 1 quart.

Orange-Pineapple Yogurt

This delicious family dessert is packed with nutrition.

1 (3-oz.) pkg. orange-flavored gelatin
1/2 cup sugar
1 cup orange juice
1 tablespoon lemon juice

1 (8-oz.) can crushed pineapple with
  juice
2 cups plain yogurt
1 cup whipping cream

In a small saucepan, combine gelatin and sugar. Stir in orange juice. Stir over medium heat until gelatin dissolves. Stir in lemon juice and pineapple with juice. In a large bowl, stir yogurt until smooth. Gradually stir in gelatin mixture. Stir in whipping cream. Pour into a 9" x 5" loaf pan. Cover with foil or plastic wrap. Freeze in freezer until firm, 3 to 6 hours. Makes about 6 cups.

Avocado-Orange Cups

An excellent luncheon dessert for avocado lovers.

3 large oranges
1 (.25-oz.) envelope unflavored gelatin
2 large ripe avocados, peeled

1/2 cup sugar
1 cup dairy sour cream
Whipped cream, if desired

Cut oranges in half crosswise. Scoop pulp from orange halves without damaging shells; reserve shells. Spoon pulp into a strainer over a small saucepan. Press juice from pulp into pan; discard pulp or use for another purpose. Reserve 1/2 cup orange juice in saucepan; use remaining juice for another purpose. Sprinkle gelatin over reserved orange juice to soften. Stir over very low heat until gelatin dissolves; set aside. Notch edges of reserved orange shells if desired; set aside. Pour gelatin mixture into blender or food processor. Cut avocados into pieces; puree with gelatin mixture. Add sugar; process 3 to 5 seconds to blend. In a small bowl, stir sour cream until smooth. Stir in avocado mixture. Spoon into reserved orange shells. Top with whipped cream, if desired. Cover with foil or plastic wrap. Place in freezer; freeze until firm, 3 to 6 hours. Makes 6 servings.

Orange Cream Sherbet   *Photo on page 117.*

Double-good orange flavor.

2 cups orange juice
3/4 cup sugar
1/2 cup orange marmalade

1 cup half-and-half
1 cup dairy sour cream

In a medium bowl, combine orange juice, sugar and marmalade. Stir in half-and-half and sour cream. Pour into a 9" x 5" loaf pan. Cover with foil or plastic wrap. Place in freezer; freeze until almost firm, 1 to 3 hours. In a chilled large bowl, beat with electric mixer until light and fluffy but not thawed. Return to pan and freeze until firm, 1 to 3 hours. Makes about 5 cups.

Golden State Sherbet

The flavor is basically orange but lemon juice adds just the right tang.

2 cups orange juice
2 tablespoons lemon juice
1-1/3 cups sugar

3 cups milk
3 or 4 drops orange food coloring

In a medium bowl, combine orange juice, lemon juice and sugar. Stir until sugar dissolves. Stir in milk and food coloring until evenly distributed. Pour into canister. Freeze in ice cream maker according to manufacturer's directions. **Freezer method:** Pour prepared mixture into a 9-inch square pan or several undivided ice trays. Cover with foil or plastic wrap. Place in freezer; freeze until firm, 3 to 6 hours. Stir 2 or 3 times while freezing. For a smoother texture, freeze prepared mixture until almost firm, 1 to 3 hours; break into small pieces. Spoon half of mixture into a chilled large bowl or chilled food processor bowl. Beat with electric mixer or metal food processor blade until light and fluffy but not thawed. Repeat with remaining frozen mixture. Return beaten mixture to pan and freeze until firm, 1 to 3 hours. Makes about 2 quarts.

Grand Marnier Cream

This will be the crowning glory to a gourmet meal.

3/4 cup sugar	8 egg yolks
1/4 cup orange juice	1/4 cup Grand Marnier liqueur
1/2 cup water	1 cup whipping cream
1 teaspoon grated orange peel	

In a small saucepan, combine sugar, orange juice, water and orange peel. Stir constantly over medium heat until mixture comes to a boil. Without stirring, boil over low heat, about 5 minutes; set aside. In a large bowl, beat egg yolks until thick and lemon colored. Beating constantly, immediately pour hot syrup in a thin stream over beaten egg yolks. Continue beating until mixture is very thick and cool. Fold in liqueur. In a small bowl, whip cream until soft peaks form. Fold into egg mixture. Spoon into a 9-inch square pan or several undivided ice trays. Cover with foil or plastic wrap. Place in freezer; freeze until firm, 3 to 6 hours. Makes about 2 quarts.

Orange Slush

Welcome the hot weather with this refreshing cooler that's so easy to make.

1 (6-oz.) can frozen orange juice concentrate	Water
	1/3 cup light corn syrup

In a 1-quart pitcher, reconstitute orange juice concentrate with water according to package directions. Stir in corn syrup until blended. Pour into canister. Freeze in ice cream maker according to manufacturer's directions. **Freezer method:** Pour prepared mixture into a 9" x 5" loaf pan. Cover with foil or plastic wrap. Place in freezer; freeze until firm, 3 to 6 hours. Scrape frozen mixture with a fork until pieces resemble finely crushed ice. Serve immediately. For a smoother texture, break frozen mixture into small pieces. Spoon into chilled food processor bowl. Beat with metal blade until smooth and fluffy but not thawed. Serve immediately. Makes 1 quart.

Frozen Lemon Cream

You'll never forget this very special lemon treat!

1/4 cup lemon juice	1/2 teaspoon grated lemon peel
1 cup sugar	2 cups half-and-half

In a medium bowl, combine lemon juice and sugar; stir to blend. Stir in lemon peel and half-and-half. Pour into a 9" x 5" loaf pan or several undivided ice trays. Cover with foil or plastic wrap. Place in freezer; freeze until firm, 3 to 6 hours. Stir with a spoon 2 or 3 times while freezing. For a smoother texture, freeze prepared mixture until almost firm, 1 to 3 hours; break into small pieces. Spoon into a chilled medium bowl. Beat with electric mixer until smooth but not thawed. Return beaten mixture to pan and freeze until firm, 1 to 3 hours. Makes about 3 cups.

Lemon Cheesecake Ice Cream

If you like cheesecake, you'll love our frozen version.

1 cup cottage cheese	1/2 teaspoon grated lemon peel
1/3 cup lemon juice	1/2 teaspoon vanilla extract
3 egg yolks	2 cups half-and-half
3/4 cup sugar	3 egg whites

In blender or food processor, puree cottage cheese and lemon juice until smooth; set aside. In a medium bowl, beat egg yolks and sugar until smooth and thick. Stir in pureed cottage-cheese mixture, lemon peel, vanilla and half-and-half; set aside. In a medium bowl, beat egg whites until stiff but not dry. Fold into egg yolk mixture. Pour into ice cream canister. Freeze in ice cream maker according to manufacturer's directions. Makes about 2 quarts.

Magic Lemon Cream

Add more lemon juice if this tastes too sweet.

1 (14-oz.) can sweetened condensed milk	1/3 cup sugar
1/3 cup lemon juice	1 cup whole milk
1/2 teaspoon grated lemon peel	

In a medium bowl, combine all ingredients. Stir until sugar dissolves. Pour into a 9" x 5" loaf pan or several undivided ice trays. Cover with foil or plastic wrap. Place in freezer; freeze until firm, 3 to 6 hours. Makes 3-1/2 to 4 cups.

Lemon Sherbet   *Photo on page 108.*

Lemon-craver's dream!

1 cup whipping cream	2 egg whites
2 tablespoons lemon juice	1/2 cup sugar
1 teaspoon grated lemon peel	

In a medium bowl, whip cream until soft peaks form. Gradually fold in lemon juice and lemon peel; set aside. In a medium bowl, beat egg whites until foamy. Gradually add sugar, beating until stiff but not dry. Fold beaten egg white mixture into whipped cream mixture. Spoon into a 9" x 5" loaf pan or several undivided ice trays. Cover with foil or plastic wrap. Place in freezer; freeze until firm, 3 to 6 hours. Stir with a fork or spoon 2 or 3 times while freezing. Makes 3 to 4 cups.

Lemon Ice

Truly refreshing frozen treat for a hot day.

4 cups water
2 cups sugar

2 teaspoons grated lemon peel
1 cup lemon juice

In a medium saucepan, combine water, sugar and lemon peel. Stir over medium heat until sugar dissolves and mixture comes to a boil. Without stirring, boil gently 5 minutes. Place a fine strainer over a medium bowl. Pour syrup through strainer to remove lemon peel; cool to room temperature. Stir in lemon juice. Pour into ice cream canister. Freeze in ice cream maker according to manufacturer's directions. **Freezer method:** Pour prepared mixture into a 9-inch square pan or several undivided ice trays. Cover with foil or plastic wrap. Place in freezer; freeze until firm, 3 to 6 hours. Scrape frozen mixture with a fork until pieces resemble finely crushed ice. Serve immediately. For a smoother texture, freeze prepared mixture until firm; break into small pieces. Spoon half of mixture into chilled food processor bowl. Beat with metal blade until light and fluffy but not thawed. Repeat with remaining frozen mixture. Serve immediately or return beaten mixture to pan and freeze until firm, 1 to 3 hours. Makes about 2 quarts.

How to Make Minty Grapefruit Sorbet

1/Cut each grapefruit in half crosswise. Remove juice by pressing and turning on a citrus reamer or juicer.

2/In a medium saucepan, stir sugar, water and mint until mixture boils. Simmer 5 minutes; cover and let stand about 10 minutes.

Lemon-Lime Freeze

Buttermilk provides a tang that complements the lemon-lime flavor.

3 eggs
2/3 cup sugar
2/3 cup light corn syrup
2 cups buttermilk

1 teaspoon grated lemon peel
2 tablespoons lemon juice
3 tablespoons lime juice
3 or 4 drops green food coloring

In a large bowl, beat eggs until blended. Gradually beat in sugar until thick and lemon colored, about 5 minutes. Beat in corn syrup, buttermilk, lemon peel, lemon juice, lime juice and food coloring until evenly distributed. Pour into ice cream canister. Freeze in ice cream maker according to manufacturer's directions. Makes about 2 quarts.

Minty Grapefruit Sorbet

There is no way to describe this fantastic flavor. You'll have to try it for yourself.

1 cup sugar
1 cup water
1 cup fresh mint leaves and stems

2 cups grapefruit juice
3 or 4 drops green food coloring

In a medium saucepan, combine sugar, water and mint. Stir over medium heat until mixture comes to a boil. Simmer over low heat 5 minutes; set aside. Cover and let stand about 10 minutes. Place a fine strainer over a large bowl. Pour syrup through strainer to remove mint; discard mint. Stir in grapefruit juice and food coloring. Pour into ice cream canister. Freeze in ice cream maker according to manufacturer's directions. **Freezer method:** Pour prepared mixture into a 9" x 5" loaf pan or several undivided ice trays. Cover with foil or plastic wrap. Place in freezer; freeze until firm, 3 to 6 hours. Stir 2 or 3 times while freezing. For a smoother texture, freeze prepared mixture until almost firm, 1 to 3 hours. Break into small pieces. Spoon into a chilled large bowl. Beat with electric mixer until smooth and fluffy but not thawed. Return beaten mixture to pan; freeze until firm, 1 to 3 hours. Makes 3 to 4 cups.

Dreamy Lime Ice Cream

Marshmallows and beaten egg whites keep this ice cream smooth and creamy.

1 cup milk
3/4 cup sugar
2 egg yolks, beaten
1/2 teaspoon grated lemon peel
1 cup miniature marshmallows

1/2 cup lime juice
1 cup whipping cream
4 or 5 drops green food coloring
2 egg whites, room temperature

In a medium saucepan, combine milk, sugar, beaten egg yolks and lemon peel. Cook and stir over low heat until mixture is thickened and coats a metal spoon; remove from heat. Stir in marshmallows until melted. Stir in lime juice, whipping cream and food coloring until evenly distributed. Pour into a 9" x 5" loaf pan or several undivided ice trays. Cover with foil or plastic wrap. Place in freezer; freeze until almost firm, 1 to 3 hours. In a small bowl, beat egg whites until stiff but not dry; set aside. Break frozen mixture into small pieces. Spoon into a chilled large bowl or chilled food processor bowl. Beat with electric mixer or metal food processor blade until smooth and fluffy but not thawed. Fold in beaten egg whites. Return beaten mixture to pan and freeze until firm, 1 to 3 hours. Makes about 1 quart.

Creamy Lime Sherbet

Deliciously smooth and tasty.

1 cup sugar
1 (.25-oz.) envelope unflavored gelatin
2 cups milk
2/3 cup lime juice

1 teaspoon grated lime peel
3 cups half-and-half
6 to 8 drops green food coloring

In a large bowl, combine sugar and gelatin; set aside. In a small saucepan, heat milk almost to boiling; pour over gelatin mixture. Stir until gelatin and sugar dissolve. Stir in lime juice and lime peel. Stir in half-and-half and food coloring until evenly distributed. Mixture will appear slightly curdled. Cool to room temperature. Pour into ice cream canister. Freeze in ice cream maker according to manufacturer's directions. Makes about 2 quarts.

1/Wash tangerines. Grate peel before cutting and squeezing fruit.

2/Peel tangerines, then pull sections apart and remove seeds.

———————————— How to Make Tangerine-Raspberry Sorbet ————————————

Tangerine-Raspberry Sorbet

Raspberry is a strong flavor. Increase the grated peel to get a stronger tangerine flavor.

1 teaspoon grated tangerine peel
5 medium tangerines
1 (10-oz.) pkg. frozen raspberries, thawed

1/2 cup light corn syrup
1/4 cup dry white wine

Grate tangerine peel; set aside. Peel tangerines and remove seeds. Combine tangerine sections, thawed raspberries and grated tangerine peel in blender or food processor. Puree until mixture is almost smooth. Place a fine strainer over a medium bowl. Pour pureed mixture into strainer; lightly press through strainer with back of a spoon to remove small pieces of pulp and raspberry seeds. Discard unstrained pulp and raspberry seeds. Stir in corn syrup and wine. Pour into ice cream canister. Freeze in ice cream maker according to manufacturer's directions. **Freezer method:** Pour prepared mixture into a 9" x 5" loaf pan or several undivided ice trays. Cover with foil or plastic wrap. Place in freezer; freeze until firm, 3 to 6 hours. Scrape frozen mixture with a fork until pieces resemble finely crushed ice. Serve immediately. For a smoother texture, freeze prepared mixture until firm, then break into small pieces. Spoon into chilled food processor bowl. Beat with metal blade until light and fluffy but not thawed. Serve immediately or return beaten mixture to pan and freeze until firm, 1 to 3 hours. Makes about 1 quart.

Tangerine-Chip Ice Cream

Melted chocolate blends but leaves flecks throughout the tangerine mixture.

6 eggs
1 cup sugar
1 tablespoon cornstarch
2 cups half-and-half
1/2 cup light corn syrup

3 cups tangerine juice
1 teaspoon grated tangerine peel
1/8 teaspoon almond extract
2 (1-oz.) squares semisweet chocolate

In a small bowl, beat eggs; set aside. In a medium saucepan, combine sugar and cornstarch. Stir in half-and-half and corn syrup. Cook and stir over low heat until thickened and bubbly. Slowly stir about 1 cup hot mixture into beaten eggs. Stir egg mixture into remaining hot mixture. Cook and stir over low heat 1 minute. Stir in tangerine juice, tangerine peel and almond extract. Cool to room temperature. Melt chocolate over hot water or in microwave. Slowly stir melted chocolate into cooled tangerine mixture. Pour into ice cream canister. Freeze in ice cream maker according to manufacturer's directions. Makes about 2 quarts.

Mandarin-Tangerine Yogurt

These two citrus flavors complement each other.

1/4 cup sugar
1 (12-oz.) can mandarin oranges,
  drained, chopped
2 cups plain yogurt

1 (6-oz.) can frozen tangerine juice
  concentrate, thawed
1/8 teaspoon almond extract

In a medium bowl, combine sugar and chopped mandarin oranges; set aside. Stir yogurt until smooth; stir into mandarin orange mixture. Stir in undiluted tangerine juice concentrate and almond extract. Pour into a 9" x 5" loaf pan. Cover with foil or plastic wrap. Place in freezer; freeze until firm, 3 to 6 hours. Stir 2 or 3 times with a fork or spoon while freezing. For a smoother texture, freeze prepared mixture until almost firm, 1 to 3 hours. Break into small pieces. Spoon into a chilled large bowl or chilled food processor bowl. Beat with electric mixer or metal food processor blade until light and fluffy but not thawed. Return beaten mixture to pan and freeze until firm, 1 to 3 hours. Makes about 1 quart.

When grating orange or lemon peel, grate only the outside, colorful layer of peel. The light part is bitter and should be discarded.

Tangerine Sherbet

Refreshing but not too rich.

1 cup sugar
1 (.25-oz.) envelope unflavored gelatin
2 cups milk
1 teaspoon grated tangerine peel

2 cups tangerine juice
1 cup half-and-half
3 or 4 drops orange food coloring,
   if desired

In a large bowl, combine sugar and gelatin; set aside. In a small saucepan, heat milk almost to boiling. Stir into gelatin mixture until gelatin and sugar dissolve. Stir in tangerine peel and tangerine juice. Stir in half-and-half and food coloring, if desired. Pour into ice cream canister. Freeze in ice cream maker according to manufacturer's directions. Makes about 6 cups.

Tangerine Sorbet

There's nothing else like the true flavor of fresh citrus juices.

2/3 cup sugar
2/3 cup light corn syrup
1 cup water

2 teaspoons grated tangerine peel
1 qt. tangerine juice
1/4 cup lemon juice

In a medium saucepan, combine sugar, corn syrup, water and tangerine peel. Stir over medium heat until sugar dissolves. Stir in tangerine juice and lemon juice. Cool to room temperature. Pour into ice cream canister. Freeze in ice cream maker according to manufacturer's directions. **Freezer method:** Pour prepared mixture into a 9-inch square pan or several undivided ice trays. Cover with foil or plastic wrap. Place in freezer; freeze until firm, 3 to 6 hours. Scrape frozen mixture with a fork until pieces resemble finely crushed ice. Serve immediately. For a smoother texture, freeze prepared mixture until firm, then break into small pieces. Spoon half of mixture into chilled food processor bowl. Beat with metal blade until light and fluffy but not thawed. Serve immediately or return beaten mixture to pan and freeze until firm, 1 to 3 hours. Makes about 2 quarts.

To have a citrus flavor without pieces of peel, add the peel to the unfrozen ice cream mixture, then pour the mixture through a fine strainer before it is frozen.

Orchard Fruits

Fresh fruit sorbets or ices will remind you of delicious just-picked ripe fruit. Fresh peaches or nectarines should be pale yellow or creamy, not green. Buy fruit that is soft to the touch if ice cream will be made today. Choose firm fruit if it won't be used for several days. Frozen desserts have a more pleasing taste and texture if the peel is removed from fresh peaches. Peel the fruit before it is pureed. Leave the peel on nectarines and plums unless flecks of peel in ice cream bother you.

Pears should be soft and ripe when used in ice creams and sorbets. Unripe fruit is more tart and the fresh-fruit flavor doesn't develop. Peel apples and pears and remove the cores before pureeing them. Applesauce, cider and apple butter are ideal ingredients for frozen desserts. They are already pureed or squeezed for you, saving time and effort. Mulled Cider Sorbet gets its old-fashioned flavor from apple juice or cider, cinnamon and cloves. The ingredients are available anytime but it's a natural treat at a Halloween party or after a Thanksgiving dinner.

Orchard fruits contain enough water naturally to puree them in a blender with little or no additional liquid. If it's a slow process getting them started, turn the blender on and off quickly several times. If the fruit packs under the blade or against the blender jar, turn off the blender and use a rubber spatula to rearrange the fruit. Once the first few pieces are pureed, there will be enough moisture for the rest to puree easily. For maximum fruit flavor and ice cream with a little texture, process fruits only until partially pureed. This will break up all pieces. No large piece of fruit will be left to bite down on when the mixture is frozen. If a finer texture is desired, puree fruits until very smooth.

Fresh Peach Ice Cream

Good old-fashioned summertime favorite.

2 eggs
1-1/4 cups sugar
1 cup milk
1/2 teaspoon vanilla extract

1/8 teaspoon almond extract
5 large, ripe peaches, peeled, chopped
1 cup whipping cream

In a large bowl, beat eggs until thick and lemon colored, about 5 minutes. Beat in sugar. Stir in milk, vanilla and almond extract; set aside. Puree peaches in blender or food processor. Stir into egg mixture. Stir in whipping cream. Pour into ice cream canister. Freeze in ice cream maker according to manufacturer's directions. Makes about 2 quarts.

Heritage Peach Ice Cream

This old-fashioned peach ice cream is made with a freezing mix.

2 cups milk
2 (4-oz.) pkgs. vanilla Junket
   Freezing Mix

1 cup whipping cream
4 fresh, large, ripe peaches, peeled

In a medium bowl, beat milk and freezing mix until mix dissolves. Stir in whipping cream; set aside. Remove and discard peach pits. Puree peaches in blender or food processor until almost smooth. Stir into milk mixture. Pour into ice cream canister. Freeze in ice cream maker according to manufacturer's directions. **Freezer method:** Pour prepared mixture into a 9-inch square pan or several undivided ice trays. Cover with foil or plastic wrap. Place in freezer; freeze until firm, 3 to 6 hours. Stir 2 or 3 times with a fork or spoon while freezing. Break into pieces; serve immediately. For a smoother texture, freeze prepared mixture until almost firm, 1 to 3 hours. Break into small pieces. Spoon half of mixture into a chilled large bowl or chilled food processor bowl. Beat with electric mixer or metal food processor blade until light and fluffy but not thawed. Repeat with remaining frozen mixture. Return beaten mixture to pan and freeze until firm, 1 to 3 hours. Makes 2 quarts.

Peach Custard Ice Cream

Delicious custard with a peach flavor.

3 eggs
1 cup sugar
1 cup milk
1/8 teaspoon almond extract

1/2 teaspoon vanilla extract
2 cups half-and-half
4 large fresh peaches, peeled

In a medium bowl, beat eggs until thick and lemon colored, about 5 minutes. Gradually beat in sugar; set aside. In a medium saucepan, combine beaten egg mixture and milk. Cook and stir over low heat until slightly thickened and mixture coats a metal spoon. Stir in almond extract, vanilla extract and half-and-half. Cool to room temperature. Remove and discard peach pits. Puree peaches in blender or food processor until almost smooth. Stir into custard mixture. Pour into ice cream canister. Freeze in ice cream maker according to manufacturer's directions. Makes about 2 quarts.

Peach Sorbet

Always select peaches at their peak of ripeness.

3/4 cup sugar
1/4 cup light corn syrup
1 cup water

8 fresh, medium, ripe peaches, peeled
2 teaspoons lemon juice

In a small saucepan, combine sugar, corn syrup and water. Bring to a boil over medium heat. Cool to room temperature. Remove and discard peach pits. Dice peaches into a large bowl. Sprinkle with lemon juice; toss to coat. Puree half of peach mixture at a time in blender or food processor. Stir into cooled syrup. Pour into ice cream canister. Freeze in ice cream maker according to manufacturer's directions. **Freezer method:** Pour prepared mixture into a 9-inch square pan or several undivided ice trays. Cover with foil or plastic wrap. Place in freezer; freeze until firm, 3 to 6 hours. Scrape frozen mixture with a fork until pieces resemble finely crushed ice. Serve immediately. For a smoother texture, freeze prepared mixture until firm; break into small pieces. Spoon half of frozen mixture into chilled food processor bowl. Beat with metal blade until light and fluffy but not thawed. Repeat with remaining frozen mixture. Serve immediately or return beaten mixture to pan and freeze until firm, 1 to 3 hours. Makes about 2 quarts.

Scoops of ice cream hold their shape longer when served in chilled dishes.

Peachy-Orange Yogurt

Substitute fresh apricots for the fresh peaches for a more tart taste.

3/4 cup sugar
1 (.25-oz.) envelope unflavored gelatin
3/4 cup light corn syrup
1 cup orange juice

5 fresh, large, ripe peaches, peeled
1 tablespoon lemon juice
3 cups plain yogurt
1 teaspoon vanilla extract

In a medium saucepan, combine sugar and gelatin. Stir in corn syrup and orange juice. Stir over low heat until sugar and gelatin dissolve. Let stand at room temperature 15 minutes. Remove and discard peach pits. Puree peaches and lemon juice in blender or food processor. Stir into partially cooled gelatin mixture. In a large bowl, stir yogurt with a whisk or spoon until smooth. Slowly stir cooled gelatin mixture into yogurt. Stir in vanilla. Pour into a 9'' x 5'' loaf pan or several undivided ice trays. Cover with foil or plastic wrap. Place in freezer; freeze until firm, 3 to 6 hours. Stir 2 or 3 times with a fork or spoon while freezing. Makes 8 to 10 servings.

Brandied Cherry Ice Cream

Delight holiday guests with this outstanding frozen dessert.

6 egg yolks
1-1/3 cups sugar
3 cups milk
2 cups whipping cream

4 cups sweet dark cherries, pitted
1/2 teaspoon almond extract
1/4 cup cherry liqueur or cherry brandy

In a small bowl, beat egg yolks until thick and lemon colored, 4 to 5 minutes. In a heavy large saucepan, combine beaten egg yolks, sugar, milk and whipping cream. Cook and stir over low heat until mixture thickens slightly and coats a metal spoon; set aside. Puree cherries in blender or food processor until almost smooth. Stir into egg mixture. Stir in almond extract and liqueur. Cool to room temperature. Pour into ice cream canister. Freeze in ice cream maker according to manufacturer's directions. Makes about 2 quarts.

Cherry Cheesecake Ice Cream

Cream cheese helps make it smooth and creamy.

1 (3-oz.) pkg. cream cheese,
   room temperature
3/4 cup milk
2 or 3 drops red food coloring, if desired

1 cup cherry preserves
1/4 teaspoon almond extract
1 cup half-and-half

In a medium bowl, beat cream cheese and milk until smooth. Stir in red food coloring, if desired, cherry preserves and almond flavoring. Stir in half-and-half. Pour into ice cream canister. Freeze in ice cream maker according to manufacturer's directions. Makes about 1 quart.

Cherries Jubilee

The cadillac of desserts! Scoop up the ice cream and marinate the cherries early in the day.

1 qt. vanilla ice cream
1 (16-oz.) can pitted dark sweet cherries,
  drained
1/4 cup orange liqueur

1/2 cup currant jelly
1 teaspoon grated orange peel
1/4 cup brandy

Three or 4 hours before serving time, scoop 6 large or 12 small ice cream balls. Place 1 large ice cream ball or 2 small ice cream balls in each of six individual serving dishes. Arrange dishes on a tray; place tray and dishes of ice cream in freezer. At same time, in a small bowl, pour liqueur over drained cherries. Marinate in refrigerator 3 or 4 hours. At serving time, in a medium skillet or chafing dish, stir jelly over low heat until melted. Stir in cherries with liqueur and orange peel. Stir over low heat until mixture begins to simmer. In a small saucepan or large metal cup, heat brandy until warm, about 150°F (65°C). **Do not let brandy get hot.** Pour warmed brandy over cherry mixture. Use a match with a long stick to ignite brandy. When flame diminishes so your fingers will not be burned, spoon cherries and sauce over frozen servings of ice cream. Serve immediately. Makes 6 servings.

Cherry-Berry Sorbet

See the variation for using canned cherries in this lovely sorbet.

4 cups fresh, ripe,
  sweet dark cherries, pitted
2/3 cup sugar

1/2 cup light corn syrup
2 cups cranberry juice

In blender or food processor, puree cherries, sugar and corn syrup until almost smooth. Add cranberry juice; process 3 to 5 seconds. Pour into ice cream canister. Freeze in ice cream maker according to manufacturer's directions. **Freezer method:** Pour prepared mixture into a 9-inch square pan or several undivided ice trays. Cover with foil or plastic wrap. Place in freezer; freeze until firm, 3 to 6 hours. Scrape frozen mixture with a fork until pieces resemble finely crushed ice. Serve immediately. For a smoother texture, freeze prepared mixture until firm; break into small pieces. Spoon half of mixture into chilled food processor bowl. Beat with metal blade until light and fluffy but not thawed. Repeat with remaining frozen mixture. Serve immediately or return beaten mixture to pan and freeze until firm, 1 to 3 hours. Makes about 2 quarts.

Variation

Substitute 2 (16-oz.) cans drained, pitted sweet dark cherries for fresh cherries. Reduce sugar to 1/2 cup.

Cherries Jubilee

Cherry-Chocolate Swirl

Tastes like a chocolate sundae.

16 large marshmallows
1/2 cup milk
1 cup whipping cream

1/2 cup chopped maraschino cherries
1/4 cup chopped pecans
1/2 cup chocolate syrup

In a medium saucepan, combine marshmallows and milk. Stir gently over low heat until marshmallows melt, about 10 minutes. Cool 10 minutes. Stir in whipping cream, cherries and pecans. Pour into a 9'' x 5'' loaf pan. Cover with foil or plastic wrap. Place in freezer; freeze until almost firm, 1 to 3 hours. Stir with a spoon. Dribble chocolate syrup over top. Use a spatula to swirl chocolate syrup back and forth through marshmallow mixture giving a marbled effect. Cover and return marbled mixture to freezer. Freeze until firm, 1 to 3 hours. Makes about 1 quart.

Tutti Frutti Sorbet

Year-round favorite made with non-seasonal fruits.

2 (12-oz.) cans apricot nectar (3 cups)
2 bananas, mashed
1/4 cup lime juice

2 (6-oz.) cans pineapple juice
  (1-1/2 cups)
1 cup sugar

In a large bowl, combine apricot nectar and mashed bananas. Stir in lime juice, pineapple juice and sugar. Pour into ice cream canister. Freeze in ice cream maker according to manufacturer's directions. **Freezer method:** Pour prepared mixture into a 9-inch square pan or several undivided ice trays. Cover with foil or plastic wrap. Place in freezer; freeze until firm, 3 to 6 hours. Scrape frozen mixture with a fork until pieces resemble finely crushed ice. Serve immediately. For a smoother texture, freeze prepared mixture until firm; break into pieces. Spoon half of mixture into chilled food processor bowl. Beat with metal blade until light and fluffy but not thawed. Repeat with remaining frozen mixture. Serve immediately or return beaten mixture to pan and freeze until firm, 1 to 3 hours. Makes about 2 quarts.

To peel a fresh peach, spear the peach with a fork. Quickly dip it into boiling water, then into cold water. Use a small knife to peel off the loosened skin.

Apricot-Lemon Cream

After it's frozen, this mixture is satiny smooth.

1 (.25-oz.) envelope unflavored gelatin
1/4 cup water
1 (29-oz.) can apricot halves, drained
1/2 cup sugar
2 cups milk

1 (6-oz.) can frozen lemonade concentrate,
 partially thawed
1 teaspoon vanilla extract
1 cup whipping cream

In a medium saucepan, sprinkle gelatin over water; set aside until softened. Puree drained apricots in blender or food processor; set aside. Stir sugar into softened gelatin. Stir in pureed apricots. Stir over medium heat until sugar and gelatin dissolve. Stir in milk, undiluted lemonade concentrate, vanilla and whipping cream. Cool to room temperature. Pour into ice cream canister. Freeze in ice cream maker according to manufacturer's directions. Makes 2 quarts.

Double Apricot Freeze

Double your pleasure with apricot halves and apricot nectar.

1 (16-oz.) can apricot halves, drained
3/4 cup apricot nectar
1/2 cup sugar

2 tablespoons lemon juice
1 cup half-and-half
2 egg whites

In blender or food processor, combine drained apricot halves, apricot nectar and sugar; puree until smooth. Add lemon juice and half-and-half. Process 2 to 3 seconds until blended. Pour into a 9" x 5" loaf pan or several undivided ice trays. Cover with foil or plastic wrap. Place in freezer; freeze until almost firm, 1 to 3 hours. Beat egg whites until stiff but not dry; set aside. Break frozen mixture into small pieces. Spoon into a chilled large bowl or chilled food processor bowl. Beat with electric mixer or metal food processor blade until smooth and fluffy but not thawed. Fold in beaten egg whites. Return beaten mixture to pan; freeze until firm, 1 to 3 hours. Makes about 1 quart.

Frozen Apricot-Pineapple Yogurt

Special easy-to-prepare treat for the whole family.

2 cups pineapple yogurt
1 cup apricot nectar
1/3 cup honey

1/8 teaspoon almond extract
2 egg whites

In a medium bowl, stir yogurt until smooth. Gradually stir in apricot nectar, honey and almond extract. Pour into a 9" x 5" loaf pan or several undivided ice trays. Cover with foil or plastic wrap. Place in freezer; freeze until nearly firm, 1 to 3 hours. Beat egg whites until stiff but not dry; set aside. Break partially frozen mixture into small pieces. Spoon into a chilled large bowl. Beat with electric mixer until light and fluffy but not thawed. Fold in beaten egg whites. Return beaten mixture to pan and freeze until firm, 1 to 3 hours. Makes about 4-1/2 cups.

Ginger-Pear Ice Cream

Use more or less ginger, depending on how strong you want the ginger flavor.

4 fresh ripe pears, peeled, cored
2 tablespoons lemon juice
3 to 4 tablespoons chopped
    crystallized ginger

1 cup sugar
2 cups milk
1 cup whipping cream

In blender or food processor, puree pears, lemon juice and ginger. Pour into a large bowl. Stir in sugar until distributed. Stir in milk, then whipping cream. Pour into ice cream canister. Freeze in ice cream maker according to manufacturer's directions. **Freezer method:** Pour prepared mixture into a 9-inch square pan or several undivided ice trays. Cover with foil or plastic wrap. Place in freezer; freeze until firm, 3 to 6 hours. Stir 2 or 3 times while freezing. For a smoother texture, freeze prepared mixture until almost firm, 1 to 3 hours. Break into small pieces. Spoon half of pieces into a chilled large bowl. Beat with electric mixer until light and fluffy but not thawed. Repeat with remaining partially frozen mixture. Return beaten mixture to pan; freeze until firm, 1 to 3 hours. Makes about 2 quarts.

Minted Pear Sorbet

Make the most of the sweet flavor of fresh pears when they are in season.

1/3 cup sugar
1/3 cup water
1/4 teaspoon grated lime peel

5 ripe pears, peeled, cored
1 tablespoon lime juice
3 tablespoons green crème de menthe liqueur

In a small saucepan, combine sugar, water and lime peel. Stir over medium heat until mixture comes to a boil; set aside to cool. Puree pears and lime juice in blender or food processor until smooth. Stir into cooled sugar mixture. Stir in crème de menthe. Pour into a 9'' x 5'' loaf pan or several undivided ice trays. Cover with foil or plastic wrap. Place in freezer; freeze until firm, 3 to 6 hours. Scrape frozen mixture with a fork until pieces resemble finely crushed ice. Serve immediately. For a smoother texture, freeze prepared mixture until firm; break into small pieces. Spoon into chilled food processor bowl. Beat with metal blade until smooth and fluffy but not thawed. Serve immediately or return beaten mixture to pan and freeze until firm, 1 to 3 hours. Makes about 1 quart.

How to Make Ginger-Pear Ice Cream

1/Crystallized ginger usually comes in pieces about the size of a large rose leaf. Cut into small pieces.

2/Use a pear cutter to cut fresh, ripe pears into eight wedges. Or use a paring knife to make wedges.

Frozen Nectarine Cream

Peel nectarines if you prefer your ice cream without flecks of peel.

2 eggs
1 cup sugar
1 cup milk
1/4 cup light corn syrup

1/2 teaspoon vanilla extract
1/8 teaspoon almond extract
5 ripe nectarines, unpeeled
1 cup whipping cream

In a large bowl, beat eggs until thick and lemon colored, about 5 minutes. Beat in sugar. Stir in milk, corn syrup, vanilla and almond extract. Remove and discard nectarine pits. Puree nectarines in blender or food processor until smooth. Stir into egg mixture. Stir in whipping cream. Pour into ice cream canister. Freeze in ice cream maker according to manufacturer's directions. Makes about 2 quarts.

Nectarine Sorbet

Chill the food processor bowl before you beat the frozen mixture in it.

2/3 cup sugar
2/3 cups light corn syrup
1 cup water

1 teaspoon grated lemon peel
2 tablespoons lemon juice
8 or 9 large ripe nectarines

In a small saucepan, combine sugar, corn syrup, water and lemon peel. Stir over medium heat until mixture comes to a boil. Stir in lemon juice. Cool to room temperature. Peel nectarines if desired; remove and discard pits. Puree nectarines in blender or food processor until smooth. Add syrup mixture; process 2 to 3 seconds to blend. Pour into ice cream canister. Freeze in ice cream maker according to manufacturer's directions. **Freezer method:** Pour prepared mixture into a 9-inch square pan or several undivided ice trays. Cover with foil or plastic wrap. Place in freezer; freeze until firm, 3 to 6 hours. Scrape frozen mixture with a fork until pieces resemble finely crushed ice. Serve immediately. For a smoother texture, freeze mixture until firm; break into pieces. Spoon half of mixture into chilled food processor bowl. Beat with metal blade until light and fluffy but not thawed. Repeat with remaining frozen mixture. Serve immediately or return beaten mixture to pan and freeze until firm, 1 to 3 hours. Makes 2 quarts.

Fresh Plum Ice Cream

Quick as a wink to prepare and enjoy.

8 fresh ripe red plums
4 eggs
1-1/3 cups sugar

2 teaspoons lemon juice
1 pt. half-and-half

Wash plums; remove and discard pits. In blender or food processor, puree half of plums with 2 eggs and 3/4 cup sugar until well blended. Pour into a large bowl. Repeat with remaining plums, eggs and sugar. Combine with previously pureed mixture. Stir in lemon juice and half-and-half. Pour into ice cream canister. Freeze in ice cream maker according to manufacturer's directions. Makes 2 quarts.

Plum Ice Italian-Style

For a change of taste, substitute peaches for the plums.

2 cups sugar
2 cups water

16 large ripe plums
2 teaspoons lemon juice

In a medium saucepan, combine sugar and water. Stir over medium heat until sugar dissolves and mixture comes to a boil. Stirring occasionally, cook to 234°F (112°C) on a candy thermometer or until mixture spins a 2-inch thread when slowly poured from a spoon. Cool at room temperature about 10 minutes. Remove and discard plum pits. Puree plums and lemon juice in blender or food processor. Place a fine strainer over a small bowl. Pour puree through strainer to remove peel, if desired. Stir pureed plums into cooled syrup. Pour into ice cream canister. Freeze in ice cream maker according to manufacturer's directions. **Freezer method:** Pour prepared mixture into a 9-inch square pan or several undivided ice trays. Cover with foil or plastic wrap. Place in freezer; freeze until firm, 3 to 6 hours. Scrape frozen mixture with a fork until pieces resemble finely crushed ice. Serve immediately. For a smoother texture, freeze prepared mixture until firm; break frozen mixture into small pieces. Spoon half of pieces into chilled food processor bowl. Beat with metal blade until light and fluffy but not thawed. Repeat with remaining frozen mixture. Serve immediately or return beaten mixture to pan and freeze until firm, 1 to 3 hours. Makes about 2 quarts.

To get their full, rich flavor, fresh fruits used in making ice cream must be fully ripe and soft but not mushy.

Fresh Plum Sorbet

Its beautiful color and fresh taste will draw compliments time and again.

1/3 cup sugar	**1/2 cup water**
1/3 cup light corn syrup	**1/2 cup orange juice**
1 teaspoon grated orange peel	**6 fresh ripe red plums**

In a small saucepan, combine sugar, corn syrup, orange peel and water. Stir over medium heat until sugar dissolves. Stir in orange juice. Cool to room temperature. Wash plums; remove and discard pits. Puree plums in blender or food processor until smooth. Place a fine strainer over a small bowl. Pour puree through strainer to remove peel, if desired. Stir strained puree into syrup mixture. Pour into ice cream canister. Freeze in ice cream maker according to manufacturer's directions. **Freezer method:** Pour prepared mixture into a 9'' x 5'' loaf pan or several undivided ice trays. Cover with foil or plastic wrap. Place in freezer; freeze until firm, 3 to 6 hours. Scrape frozen mixture with a fork until pieces resemble finely crushed ice. Serve immediately. For a smoother texture, freeze prepared mixture until firm; break into small pieces. Spoon into chilled food processor bowl. Beat with metal blade until light and fluffy but not thawed. Serve immediately or return beaten mixture to pan and freeze until firm, 1 to 3 hours. Makes about 1 quart.

Pomegranate Sorbet

Its spectacular color and good taste ensure universal appeal.

1-1/2 cups water	**3 fresh medium pomegranates**
1/3 cup sugar	**2 tablespoons lemon juice**
1/3 cup light corn syrup	

In a small saucepan, combine water, sugar and corn syrup. Stir over medium heat until sugar dissolves; set aside. Cool to room temperature. Cut pomegranates in half crosswise. Press and turn on an orange reamer to remove juice. Reserve juice; discard pulp, seeds and peel. There will be about 1 cup pomegranate juice. Stir pomegranate juice and lemon juice into cooled syrup. Pour into ice cream canister. Freeze in ice cream maker according to manufacturer's directions. **Freezer method:** Pour prepared mixture into a 9'' x 5'' loaf pan or several undivided ice trays. Cover with foil or plastic wrap. Place in freezer; freeze until firm, 3 to 6 hours. Scrape frozen mixture with a fork until pieces resemble finely crushed ice. Serve immediately. For a smoother texture, freeze prepared mixture until firm; break into small pieces. Spoon into chilled food processor bowl. Beat with metal blade until light and fluffy but not thawed. Serve immediately or return beaten mixture to pan and freeze until firm, 1 to 3 hours. Makes about 1 quart.

Apple-Cheese Ice Cream

This flavor combination is a favorite among the Pennsylvania Dutch.

5 cooking apples, peeled, cored
2 cups cottage cheese
1 cup half-and-half
1/2 cup apple butter

1/2 cup sugar
1/2 teaspoon ground cinnamon
1/4 teaspoon ground cloves
2 eggs

Chop apples into 1/8- to 1/4-inch pieces; set aside. In blender or food processor, combine 1 cup cottage cheese, 1/2 cup half-and-half, 1/4 cup apple butter, 1/4 cup sugar, cinnamon, cloves and one egg. Blend until smooth. Pour into a large bowl. Repeat with remaining cottage cheese, half-and-half, apple butter and egg. Combine with previously pureed mixture. Stir in chopped apples. Pour into ice cream canister. Freeze in ice cream maker according to manufacturer's directions. Makes about 2 quarts.

—————————— How to Make Pomegranate Sorbet ——————————

1/Cut pomegranate in half crosswise. Remove juice by pressing and turning on a citrus reamer or juicer. Discard pulp and seeds.

2/When sorbet is almost frozen solid, beat chunks in food processor until light and fluffy; serve immediately or return to freezer.

Candy-Apple Ice Cream

Cinnamon-flavored red hots give a heavenly color and flavor.

4 medium cooking apples, peeled, cored
1/3 cup red cinnamon candies
1/2 cup water

1 cup light corn syrup
2 cups half-and-half

Cut apples into chunks. In a medium saucepan, combine apples, cinnamon candies, water and corn syrup. Cook and stir over medium heat until apples are tender and candies melt. In blender or food processor, puree apple mixture until almost smooth. Cool to room temperature. Stir in half and half. Pour into ice cream canister. Freeze in ice cream maker according to manufacturer's directions. Makes about 2 quarts.

Apple-Walnut Custard

Sugar and spice and everything nice!

2 cups milk
1/2 cup packed brown sugar
2 eggs, beaten
1/2 teaspoon ground cinnamon
1/4 teaspoon ground nutmeg

4 tart cooking apples, peeled, cored
1/2 cup light corn syrup
1 tablespoon lemon juice
1 cup whipping cream
1/3 cup chopped walnuts

In a small saucepan, combine milk, brown sugar and beaten eggs. Cook and stir over low heat until mixture thickens slightly and coats a metal spoon. Stir in cinnamon and nutmeg; cool to room temperature. Cut apples into pieces. Puree apple pieces, corn syrup and lemon juice in blender or food processor until almost smooth. In a large bowl, combine pureed apple mixture, cooled custard, whipping cream and walnuts. Pour into ice cream canister. Freeze in ice cream maker according to manufacturer's directions. Makes about 2 quarts.

1/In a medium saucepan, cook and stir apple chunks, cinnamon candies, water and corn syrup until apples are tender and candies dissolve.

2/In blender or food processor, puree apple mixture until almost smooth; cool. Stir in half-and-half. Pour into ice cream canister.

How to Make Candy-Apple Ice Cream

Mulled Cider Sorbet

This captures the delicious flavor of mulled cider.

5 cups apple juice or apple cider
2 whole cinnamon sticks
8 whole cloves

1 cup sugar
1 cup orange juice
2 tablespoons lemon juice

In a large saucepan, combine apple juice or apple cider, cinnamon sticks, whole cloves and sugar. Stir over medium heat until sugar dissolves. Stirring occasionally, bring to a boil. Continue stirring over medium heat 5 minutes. With a slotted spoon, remove and discard cinnamon sticks and cloves. Stir in orange juice and lemon juice. Cool to room temperature. Pour into ice cream canister. Freeze in ice cream maker according to manufacturer's directions. **Freezer method:** Pour prepared mixture into a 9-inch square pan or several undivided ice trays. Cover with foil or plastic wrap. Place in freezer; freeze until firm, 3 to 6 hours. Scrape frozen mixture with a fork until pieces resemble finely crushed ice. Serve immediately. For a smoother texture, freeze prepared mixture until firm; break into small pieces. Spoon half of mixture into chilled food processor bowl. Beat with metal blade until smooth and fluffy but not thawed. Repeat with remaining frozen mixture. Serve immediately or return beaten mixture to pan and freeze until firm, 1 to 3 hours. Makes about 2 quarts.

Frozen Apple Yogurt

Quick and easy to put together.

4 cups plain yogurt
1 cup apple butter
1/2 cup sugar

1/2 cup light corn syrup
1/4 teaspoon ground cinnamon

In a large bowl, stir yogurt with a wisk or spoon until smooth. Stir in apple butter, sugar, corn syrup, and cinnamon until sugar dissolves. Pour into ice cream canister. Freeze in ice cream maker according to manufacturer's directions. **Freezer method:** Pour prepared mixture into a 9-inch square pan or several undivided ice trays. Cover with foil or plastic wrap. Place in freezer; freeze until partially frozen, 1 to 3 hours. Stir with a spoon or fork, then freeze until firm, 1 to 3 hours. Makes about 2 quarts.

Spicy Applesauce Freeze

Delicate apple flavor laced with your favorite spices.

1 (.25-oz.) envelope unflavored gelatin
1 (14-oz.) jar unsweetened applesauce
3/4 cup lightly packed brown sugar
2 eggs, beaten
1/2 teaspoon ground cinnamon

1/4 teaspoon ground mace
1/8 teaspoon ground ginger
1 cup dairy sour cream
2 cups half-and-half

In a small saucepan, sprinkle gelatin over applesauce. Stir to blend; set aside about 5 minutes. Stir in brown sugar, beaten eggs, cinnamon, mace and ginger. Cook and stir over low heat until gelatin dissolves and mixture thickens slightly. Cool to lukewarm. Stir in sour cream and half-and-half. Pour into ice cream canister. Freeze in ice cream maker according to manufacturer's directions. **Freezer method:** Pour prepared mixture into a 9-inch square pan or several undivided ice trays. Cover with foil or plastic wrap. Place in freezer; freeze until firm, 3 to 6 hours. Stir 2 or 3 times with a fork or spoon while freezing. For a smoother texture, freeze prepared mixture until almost firm, 1 to 3 hours. Break into small pieces. Spoon half of mixture into a chilled large bowl or chilled food processor bowl. Beat with electric mixer or metal food processor blade until light and fluffy but not thawed. Repeat with remaining frozen mixture. Return beaten mixture to pan and freeze until firm, 1 to 3 hours. Makes about 2 quarts.

Sprinkle the cut sides of fresh apples, pears or peaches with lemon juice to prevent darkening.

Tropical Fruits

You'll imagine yourself on a lush island, sitting under a palm tree with cool breezes brushing over you as you taste these exotic tropical ice creams and sorbets. With fresh, frozen or dried fruit or tropical fruit juices from supermarkets, you can make these mixtures any time.

Don't wander any farther than your backyard to create the mystical charm of the tropics. At your next backyard barbecue, plan a luau topped off with one of our tropical ice creams or sorbets. Start one or two days ahead and make several flavors and colors. Present four or five servings in a fresh scooped-out pineapple half on a flower-covered tray. Display individual servings in papaya or orange peel halves arranged on serving plates decorated with ferns or fresh flowers.

Bananas are the most popular and best-known tropical fruit. Fresh bananas are available all year and have become a requested ice cream flavor. Use only ripe bananas with bright yellow peel flecked with brown. The fruit should be slightly soft to the touch. If bananas at your local supermarket are usually green, buy them several days before making ice cream and let them ripen at room temperature. Puree bananas with lemon or lime juice to prevent darkening.

Fresh coconut, growing in popularity as an ice cream flavor, is also available most of the year. The fresh flavor is enticing, but it takes time to open the shell and grate the fruit. Ready-to-use flaked coconut is available in small cans or plastic bags. Cream of coconut, a fairly thick syrup, is often used in mixing tropical drinks. You'll find 16-ounce cans in the beverage department of supermarkets. It has a definite coconut flavor without small shreds or flakes of coconut in it.

Bali Hai Cream

Enjoy this frozen beauty from the tropics on any hot day.

1 large banana	1 cup pineapple juice
1 tablespoon lemon juice	1/2 cup flaked coconut
2 eggs	1/8 teaspoon almond extract
1/2 cup sugar	1 cup whipping cream

Cut banana into chunks. In blender or food processor, puree banana and lemon juice until almost smooth. In a medium bowl, beat eggs and sugar until thick and smooth. Stir in pureed banana, pineapple juice, coconut, almond extract and whipping cream. Pour into ice cream canister. Freeze in ice cream maker according to manufacturer's directions. **Freezer method:** Pour prepared mixture into a 9-inch square pan or several undivided ice trays. Cover with foil or plastic wrap. Place in freezer; freeze until firm, 3 to 6 hours. Stir 2 or 3 times with a fork or spoon while freezing. For a smoother texture, freeze until almost firm, 1 to 3 hours. Break into small pieces. Spoon half of mixture into a large chilled bowl or chilled food processor bowl. Beat with electric mixer or metal food processor blade until light and fluffy but not thawed. Repeat with remaining partially frozen mixture. Immediately return beaten mixture to pan and freeze until firm, 1 to 3 hours. Makes about 2 quarts.

Peanut-Butter Banana Ice Cream

Peanut butter fans will always ask for seconds on this one.

2 eggs	1 tablespoon lemon juice
1/2 cup sugar	2 cups half-and-half
1/4 cup light corn syrup	1 cup whipping cream
2 medium bananas, mashed	1/4 cup peanut butter

In a large bowl, beat eggs until blended. Beat in sugar and corn syrup until smooth and light. Beat in mashed bananas and lemon juice until blended. Beat in half-and-half, whipping cream and peanut butter. Pour into ice cream canister. Freeze in ice cream maker according to manufacturer's directions. **Freezer method:** Pour prepared mixture into a 9-inch square pan or several undivided ice trays. Cover with foil or plastic wrap. Place in freezer; freeze until firm, 3 to 6 hours. Stir 2 or 3 times with a fork or spoon while freezing. For a smoother texture, freeze until almost firm, 1 to 3 hours. Break into small pieces. Spoon into a chilled large bowl or chilled food processor bowl. Beat with electric mixer or metal food processor blade until light and fluffy but not thawed. Repeat with remaining partially frozen mixture. Immediately return beaten mixture to pan and freeze until firm, 1 to 3 hours. Makes about 2 quarts.

To toast coconut, spread a thin layer of flaked coconut on a shallow baking pan. Bake in a 350°F (175°C) oven 5 to 7 minutes or until golden.

Banana-Orange Yogurt

Attention all yogurt fans! This one is a hit!

2 large bananas, mashed
1 tablespoon lemon juice
1/2 cup honey

1 cup orange juice
2 cups plain yogurt

In a large bowl, combine mashed bananas, lemon juice, honey and orange juice. Stir yogurt until smooth, then stir into banana mixture. Pour into ice cream canister. Freeze in ice cream maker according to manufacturer's directions. Makes about 6 cups.

Banana-Rum Ice Cream

You'll enjoy these frozen Caribbean flavors.

2 eggs
1/2 cup sugar
1/4 cup honey
2 medium bananas, mashed

1 tablespoon lemon juice
2 cups half-and-half
1 cup whipping cream
3 tablespoons rum

In a large bowl, beat eggs until blended. Beat in sugar and honey until smooth and light. Stir in bananas and lemon juice. Stir in half-and-half, whipping cream and rum. Pour into ice cream canister. Freeze in ice cream maker according to manufacturer's directions. Makes about 2 quarts.

Banana-Macadamia-Nut Ice Cream

Very rich but very, very good!

1 cup sugar
1 tablespoon cornstarch
1 cup half-and-half
1 cup milk
3 eggs, slightly beaten
1 cup whipping cream

1 teaspoon vanilla extract
2 medium bananas, mashed
1 tablespoon lemon juice
2-1/2 oz. macadamia nuts,
    finely chopped (1/2 cup)

In a medium saucepan, combine sugar and cornstarch. Stir in half-and-half and milk. Cook and stir over low heat until mixture thickens slightly. Simmer 1 minute longer to cook cornstarch. Stir 1 cup hot cornstarch mixture into beaten eggs. Stir egg mixture into remaining cornstarch mixture. Cook and stir 2 minutes until smooth and thickened. Stir in whipping cream, vanilla, mashed bananas, lemon juice and nuts. Cool to room temperature. Pour into ice cream canister. Freeze in ice cream maker according to manufacturer's directions. Makes about 2 quarts.

Banana-Orange Sorbet

Like most sorbets, this one is at its best when eaten as soon as it is frozen.

2/3 cup sugar	2 cups orange juice
2/3 cup light corn syrup	4 large ripe bananas, cut in pieces
1 cup water	1/4 cup orange liqueur, if desired

In a small saucepan, combine sugar, corn syrup and water. Stir over low heat until sugar dissolves. Stir in orange juice; set aside. Puree bananas in blender or food processor. Stir into orange juice mixture. Stir in liqueur, if desired. Pour into ice cream canister. Freeze in ice cream maker according to manufacturer's directions. **Freezer method:** Pour prepared mixture into a 9-inch square pan or several undivided ice trays. Cover with foil or plastic wrap. Place in freezer; freeze until firm, 3 to 6 hours. Stir 2 or 3 times with a fork or spoon while freezing. Scrape frozen mixture with a fork until pieces resemble finely crushed ice. Serve immediately. For a smoother texture, freeze until firm; break into small pieces. Spoon half of mixture into chilled food processor bowl. Beat with metal blade until light and fluffy but not thawed. Repeat with remaining frozen mixture. Serve immediately or return beaten mixture to pan and freeze until firm, 1 to 3 hours. Makes about 2 quarts.

Beachcomber's Delight

Coconut adds the finishing touch to this tropical flavor treat.

4 egg yolks	1/8 teaspoon ground mace
1 cup milk	1 (8-oz.) can crushed pineapple in
1 cup half-and-half	unsweetened juice
3/4 cup sugar	1 cup whipping cream
2 ripe papayas, peeled	1/4 cup flaked coconut

In a medium bowl, beat egg yolks until thick and lemon colored, about 5 minutes. In a heavy large saucepan, combine beaten egg yolks, milk, half-and-half and sugar. Cook and stir over low heat until mixture is slightly thickened and coats a metal spoon. Set aside to cool. Remove and discard papayas seeds. Process papayas and mace in blender or food processor until almost smooth. Stir pureed papaya mixture and pineapple with juice into cooled custard. Stir in whipping cream and coconut. Cool to room temperature. Pour into ice cream canister. Freeze in ice cream maker according to manufacturer's directions. **Freezer method:** Pour prepared mixture into a 9-inch square pan or several undivided ice trays. Cover with foil or plastic wrap. Place in freezer; freeze until firm, 3 to 6 hours. Stir 2 or 3 times while freezing. For a smoother texture, freeze until almost firm, 1 to 3 hours. Break into small pieces. Spoon half of mixture into a chilled large bowl or chilled food processor bowl. Beat with electric mixer or metal food processor blade until light and fluffy but not thawed. Repeat with remaining partially frozen mixture. Immediately return beaten mixture to pan and freeze until firm, 1 to 3 hours. Makes about 2 quarts.

Clockwise from right, Papaya filled with Coco-Damia Ice Cream, page 87; Coconut filled with Mango-Coconut Yogurt, page 86; Pineapple filled with Kiwi Ice Cream, page 89 and Trade Winds Sorbet, page 84.

Papaya Ice Cream

Brings the flavor of Hawaii to your table.

2 ripe papayas, peeled	3 eggs
2 tablespoons lemon juice	1 cup half-and-half
3/4 cup sugar	1 cup whipping cream

Remove and discard papaya seeds. Puree papaya and lemon juice in blender or food processor until almost smooth; add sugar and eggs. Process 3 to 5 seconds or until blended. In a large bowl, combine pureed mixture, half-and-half and whipping cream. Pour into ice cream canister. Freeze in ice cream maker according to manufacturer's directions. **Freezer method:** Pour prepared mixture into a 9-inch square pan or several undivided ice trays. Cover with foil or plastic wrap. Place in freezer; freeze until firm, 3 to 6 hours. Stir 2 or 3 times with a fork or spoon while freezing. For a smoother texture, freeze until almost firm, 1 to 3 hours. Break into small pieces. Spoon half of mixture into a chilled large bowl or chilled food processor bowl. Beat with electric mixer or metal food processor blade until light and fluffy but not thawed. Repeat with remaining partially frozen mixture. Immediately return beaten mixture to pan and freeze until firm, 1 to 3 hours. Makes about 2 quarts.

Trade Winds Sorbet   *Photo on page 82.*

Tropical flavors at their best.

2 cups water	1 (16-oz.) can crushed pineapple
1/2 cup sugar	with juice
1/2 cup light corn syrup	2 tablespoons lemon juice
2 large ripe mangoes	

In a medium saucepan, combine water, sugar and corn syrup. Stir over low heat until sugar dissolves. Set aside and cool to room temperature. Peel mangoes. Cut pulp from seeds; discard seeds. In blender or food processor, puree mango pulp, crushed pineapple with juice and lemon juice until mixture is almost smooth. Stir into cooled syrup. Pour into ice cream canister. Freeze in ice cream maker according to manufacturer's directions. **Freezer method:** Pour prepared mixture into a 9-inch square pan or several undivided ice trays. Cover with foil or plastic wrap. Place in freezer; freeze until almost firm, 1 to 3 hours. Break into small pieces. Spoon half of mixture into chilled food processor bowl or a chilled large bowl. Beat with metal food processor blade or with electric mixer until light and fluffy but not thawed. Repeat with remaining partially frozen mixture. Immediately return beaten mixture to pan and freeze until firm, 1 to 3 hours. Makes about 2 quarts.

1/Peel papaya. Cut fruit in half; scoop out and discard papaya seeds. Cut into large pieces before blending.

2/Puree papaya and lemon juice in blender until mixture is slightly lumpy. Puree longer for a smoother texture.

How to Make Papaya Ice Cream

Mango Sorbet

Refreshing as a Hawaiian breeze.

3 cups water
2/3 cup sugar
2/3 cup light corn syrup

2 large ripe mangoes
1 cup orange juice
1/4 cup orange liqueur

In a medium saucepan, combine water, sugar and corn syrup. Stir over medium heat until sugar dissolves; set aside to cool. Peel mangoes. Cut pulp from seeds; discard seeds. Puree mango pulp and orange juice in blender or food processor until almost smooth. Stir into cooled syrup. Stir in liqueur. Pour into ice cream canister. Freeze in ice cream maker according to manufacturer's directions. **Freezer method:** Pour prepared mixture into a 9-inch square pan or several undivided ice trays. Cover with foil or plastic wrap. Place in freezer; freeze until firm, 3 to 6 hours. Scrape frozen mixture with a fork until pieces resemble finely crushed ice. Serve immediately. For a smoother texture, freeze until firm; break into small pieces. Spoon half of mixture into chilled food processor bowl. Beat with metal blade until light and fluffy but not thawed. Repeat with remaining frozen mixture. Serve immediately or return beaten mixture to pan and freeze until firm, 1 to 3 hours. Makes about 2 quarts.

Mango Ice Cream

Smooth and creamy with a flavor from the South Pacific.

2 ripe mangoes	**3/4 cup sugar**
2 tablespoons lemon juice	**3 cups half-and-half**
2 egg yolks	**1/8 teaspoon almond extract**

Peel mangoes. Cut pulp from seeds; discard seeds. Puree mango pulp and lemon juice in blender or food processor; set aside. In a large bowl, beat egg yolks and sugar until light and fluffy. Stir in pureed mixture, half-and-half and almond extract. Pour into ice cream canister. Freeze in ice cream maker according to manufacturer's directions. Makes about 2 quarts.

Mango-Coconut Yogurt   *Photo on page 82.*

So good! And good for you, too.

2 ripe mangoes	**4 cups plain yogurt**
1 cup honey	**1/2 cup flaked coconut**

Peel mangoes. Cut pulp from seeds; discard seeds. In blender or food processor, puree mango pulp and honey until almost smooth; set aside. In a large bowl, stir yogurt until smooth. Stir in pureed fruit mixture and coconut. Pour into ice cream canister. Freeze in ice cream maker according to manufacturer's directions. **Freezer method:** Pour prepared mixture into a 9-inch square pan or several undivided ice trays. Cover with foil or plastic wrap. Place in freezer; freeze until firm, 3 to 6 hours. Stir 2 or 3 times with a fork or spoon while freezing. For a smoother texture, freeze until almost firm, 1 to 3 hours. Break into small pieces. Spoon half of mixture into a chilled large bowl or chilled food processor bowl. Beat with electric mixer or metal food processor blade until light and fluffy but not thawed. Repeat with remaining partially frozen mixture. Immediately return beaten mixture to pan and freeze until firm, 1 to 3 hours. Makes about 2 quarts.

Anytime Tropical Freeze

Ingredients are available year-round so you can make it anytime.

3 medium bananas	**2 tablespoons lemon juice**
1 (6-oz.) can orange juice concentrate, partially thawed	**1/4 cup sugar**
	1/2 teaspoon vanilla extract
1 (8-oz.) can crushed pineapple with juice	**1/2 cup half-and-half**

In a large bowl, mash bananas. Stir in orange juice concentrate, pineapple with juice, lemon juice, sugar and vanilla. Stir in half-and-half. Pour into a 9'' x 5'' loaf pan or several undivided ice trays. Cover with foil or plastic wrap. Place in freezer; freeze until almost firm, 1 to 3 hours. Spoon into a chilled large bowl. Beat with electric mixer until light and fluffy but not thawed. Immediately return beaten mixture to pan and freeze until firm, 1 to 3 hours. Makes about 1 quart.

Coco-Damia Ice Cream *Photo on page 82.*

An unbeatable flavor combination of coconut and macadamia nuts.

1 cup chopped macadamia nuts	**2 teaspoons vanilla extract**
1 tablespoon butter or margarine	**1/2 cup milk**
2 eggs	**1 cup whipping cream**
1-1/2 cups sugar	**2 cups half-and-half**
1/4 teaspoon salt	**1 cup flaked coconut**

In a small skillet, sauté nuts in butter until lightly browned, 3 to 5 minutes. Set aside to cool. In a large bowl, beat eggs until thick and lemon colored. Add sugar, salt, vanilla and milk. Beat at medium speed with electric mixer until sugar is dissolved. Stir in whipping cream, half-and-half, flaked coconut and sautéed nuts. Pour into ice cream canister. Freeze in ice cream maker according to manufacturer's directions. **Freezer method:** Pour prepared mixture into a 9-inch square pan or several undivided ice cube trays. Cover with foil or plastic wrap. Place in freezer; freeze until firm, 3 to 6 hours. Stir 2 or 3 times with a fork or spoon while freezing. For a smoother texture, freeze until almost firm, 1 to 3 hours. Spoon half of mixture into a chilled large bowl or chilled food processor bowl. Beat with electric mixer or metal food processor blade until light and fluffy but not thawed. Repeat with remaining frozen mixture. Immediately return beaten mixture to pan and freeze until firm, 1 to 3 hours. Makes about 2 quarts.

Coconut Sherbet

Hold the frozen mixture overnight in the freezer for a more definite coconut flavor.

2 (3-1/2-oz.) cans flaked coconut	**1/2 cup sugar**
1 (13-oz.) can evaporated milk	**1/4 cup light corn syrup**
1 (.25-oz.) envelope unflavored gelatin	**3 cups whole milk**

In blender, combine coconut and evaporated milk. Process until coconut is in very tiny pieces. Pour into a medium saucepan. Sprinkle gelatin over top; stir to soften. Stir in sugar and corn syrup. Stir over medium heat until gelatin dissolves. Place a fine strainer over a large bowl. Pour coconut mixture into strainer. With back of spoon, push as much of coconut mixture through strainer as possible. Discard remaining coconut. Stir whole milk into coconut mixture. Pour into ice cream canister. Freeze in ice cream maker according to manufacturer's directions. **Freezer method:** Pour prepared mixture into a 9" x 5" loaf pan or several undivided ice trays. Cover with foil or plastic wrap. Place in freezer; freeze until firm, 3 to 6 hours. Stir 2 or 3 times with a fork or spoon while freezing. For a smoother texture, freeze until almost firm, 1 to 3 hours. Break into small pieces. Spoon into a chilled large bowl or spoon half of mixture into chilled food processor bowl. Beat with electric mixer or metal food processor blade until light and fluffy but not thawed. Repeat with remaining mixture if necessary. Immediately return beaten mixture to pan and freeze until firm, 1 to 3 hours. Makes about 1-1/2 quarts.

1/Peel ripe kiwi with a knife. Cut into halves or quarters before blending. It is not necessary to strain seeds.

2/Finished ice cream should be pale green, speckled with tiny seeds. Garnish with extra slices of kiwi.

How to Make Kiwi Ice Cream

Cream of Coconut Freeze

Cream of coconut is a thick coconut syrup often used in making tropical drinks.

4 eggs, beaten
1 (16-oz.) can cream of coconut
2 cups milk

1 teaspoon vanilla extract
1 cup whipping cream
1 cup half-and-half

In a medium saucepan, combine beaten eggs, cream of coconut and milk. Cook and stir over low heat until mixture thickens and coats a metal spoon. Stir in vanilla, whipping cream and half-and-half. Cool to room temperature. Pour into ice cream canister. Freeze in ice cream maker according to manufacturer's directions. **Freezer method:** Pour prepared mixture into a 9-inch square pan or several undivided ice trays. Cover with foil or plastic wrap. Place in freezer; freeze until firm, 3 to 6 hours. Stir 2 or 3 times with a fork or spoon while freezing. For a smoother texture, freeze until almost firm, 1 to 3 hours. Break into small pieces. Spoon half of mixture into a chilled large bowl or chilled food processor bowl. Beat with electric mixer or metal food processor blade until light and fluffy but not thawed. Repeat with remaining partially frozen mixture. Immediately return beaten mixture to pan and freeze until firm, 1 to 3 hours. Makes about 2 quarts.

Kiwi Ice Cream   *Photo on page 82.*

For maximum flavor, make sure the kiwi fruit is ripe.

4 ripe kiwi, peeled
2/3 cup orange juice
2 eggs
1-1/2 cups sugar

2 cups whipping cream
1/2 teaspoon vanilla extract
6 to 8 drops green food coloring

In blender or food processor, puree kiwi and orange juice until almost smooth; set aside. In a large bowl, beat eggs and sugar until smooth and thick. Stir in pureed mixture, whipping cream, vanilla and food coloring until evenly distributed. Pour into ice cream canister. Freeze in ice cream maker according to manufacturer's directions. **Freezer method:** Pour prepared mixture into a 9-inch square pan or several undivided ice trays. Cover with foil or plastic wrap. Place in freezer; freeze until firm, 3 to 6 hours. Stir 2 or 3 times with a fork or spoon while freezing. For a smoother texture, freeze until almost firm, 1 to 3 hours. Break into small pieces. Spoon half of mixture into a large chilled bowl or chilled food processor bowl. Beat with electric mixer or metal food processor blade until light and fluffy but not thawed. Repeat with remaining partially frozen mixture. Immediately return beaten mixture to pan and freeze until firm, 1 to 3 hours. Makes about 2 quarts.

Kiwi Sorbet

Serve this delightfully refreshing, pale-green sorbet on any occasion.

1 cup sugar
1 cup light corn syrup
2 cups water

6 kiwi, peeled
1/4 cup lemon juice

In a medium saucepan, combine sugar, corn syrup and water. Stir over medium heat until sugar dissolves; set aside. Puree kiwi and lemon juice in blender or food processor until almost smooth. Stir into syrup. Pour into ice cream canister. Freeze in ice cream maker according to manufacturer's direction. **Freezer method:** Pour prepared mixture into a 9-inch square pan or several undivided ice trays. Cover with foil or plastic wrap. Place in freezer; freeze until almost firm, 1 to 3 hours. Spoon half of mixture into chilled food processor bowl or into a chilled large bowl. Beat with metal food processor blade or with electric mixer until light and fluffy but not thawed. Repeat with remaining partially frozen mixture. Immediately return beaten mixture to pan and freeze until firm, 1 to 3 hours. Makes about 2 quarts.

Mai Tai Ice

This is a frozen version of the ever-popular Hawaiian drink.

1/4 fresh ripe pineapple
2 cups Mai Tai mix
1/4 cup rum
Fresh pineapple spears for decoration,
   if desired

Maraschino cherries for decoration,
   if desired

Peel and core pineapple; cut fruit into pieces. In blender or food processor, process pineapple pieces until finely chopped. Pour into a medium bowl. Stir in Mai Tai mix and rum. Pour into a 9" x 5" loaf pan or several undivided ice trays. Cover with foil or plastic wrap. Place in freezer; freeze until firm, 3 to 6 hours. For slightly icy texture, scrape frozen mixture with a fork until pieces resemble finely crushed ice. For a smoother texture, freeze until firm; break into small pieces. Spoon pieces into chilled food processor bowl. Beat with metal blade until light and fluffy but not thawed. Serve immediately or return beaten mixture to pan and freeze until firm, 1 to 3 hours. To serve, spoon into sherbet glasses. Decorate with pineapple spears and maraschino cherries, if desired. Makes 4 to 5 servings or about 3-1/2 cups.

Date-Nut Ice Cream

For a more pronounced date flavor, chop whole dates instead of using packaged chopped dates.

2 tablespoons butter or margarine
1/2 cup chopped walnuts
1 (.25-oz.) envelope unflavored gelatin
2 cups milk

1/2 cup honey
1 cup chopped pitted dates
1/2 teaspoon vanilla extract
1 cup whipping cream

In a small skillet, melt butter or margarine. Add nuts; stir over medium heat until nuts are golden brown. Set aside to cool. In a medium saucepan, sprinkle gelatin over milk; stir until gelatin is softened. Stir in honey and dates. Cook and stir over low heat until mixture begins to simmer and thicken; cool to room temperature. Stir in browned nuts, vanilla and whipping cream. Pour into ice cream canister. Freeze in ice cream maker according to manufacturer's directions. Makes about 6 cups.

Sun-Date Yogurt

Made with natural ingredients; loaded with good nutrition.

2 cups plain yogurt
1/2 cup chopped dates

1/2 cup sunflower seeds
1/2 cup honey

In a medium bowl, stir yogurt until smooth. Stir in dates, sunflower seeds and honey. Pour into ice cream canister. Freeze in ice cream maker according to manufacturer's directions. **Freezer method:** Pour prepared mixture into a 9" x 5" loaf pan or several undivided ice trays. Cover with foil or plastic wrap. Place in freezer; freeze until firm, 3 to 6 hours. Stir 2 or 3 times with a fork or spoon while freezing. Makes about 1 quart.

Hawaiian Sorbet

Your guests will be delighted with this smooth and fruity sorbet.

2 cups water	**2 cups orange juice**
1 cup sugar	**2 tablespoons lemon juice**
1/2 fresh pineapple	

In a medium saucepan, combine water and sugar. Stir over low heat until sugar dissolves. Bring to a boil. Boil gently 5 minutes without stirring; set aside. Peel and core pineapple; cut fruit into pieces. Puree pineapple pieces in blender or food processor until almost smooth. Stir pureed pineapple, orange juice and lemon juice into syrup; cool to room temperature. Pour into ice cream canister. Freeze in ice cream maker according to manufacturer's directions. **Freezer method:** Pour prepared mixture into a 9-inch square pan or several undivided ice trays. Cover with foil or plastic wrap. Place in freezer; freeze until firm, 3 to 6 hours. Scrape frozen mixture with a fork until pieces resemble finely crushed ice. For a smoother texture, freeze until firm; break into small pieces. Spoon half of mixture into chilled food processor bowl. Beat with metal blade until light and fluffy but not thawed. Repeat with remaining frozen mixture. Serve immediately or return beaten mixture to pan and freeze until firm, 1 to 3 hours. Makes about 2 quarts.

Ports of Call Sorbet

Stir this sorbet during the freezing process to keep the fruits evenly distributed.

1/2 cup sugar	**1 (8-oz.) can crushed pineapple with**
1/2 cup light corn syrup	**juice**
1 cup water	**1 cup orange juice**
1 large banana	**2 tablespoons lime juice**

In a small saucepan, combine sugar, corn syrup and water. Stir over medium heat until sugar dissolves; set aside. In a medium bowl, mash banana. Stir in pineapple with juice, orange juice and lime juice. Stir in syrup. Pour into a 9'' x 5'' loaf pan or several undivided ice trays. Cover with foil or plastic wrap. Place in freezer; freeze until almost firm, 1 to 3 hours. Stir 2 or 3 times with a fork or spoon while freezing. Makes about 1 quart.

To have pieces of tropical fruits in ice cream, finely chop or mash the fruit with an electric mixer rather than pureeing them.

Avo-Orange Ice Cream

For maximum flavor and smooth texture, be sure the avocados are ripe.

2 large ripe avocados, peeled
1 (6-oz.) can frozen orange juice
  concentrate, partially thawed

1 tablespoon lemon juice
3/4 cup sugar
2 cups half-and-half

Cut avocados into pieces. In blender or food processor, puree avocado pieces, undiluted orange juice concentrate, lemon juice and sugar until smooth. Add half-and-half; process 1 to 2 seconds to blend. Pour into a 9" x 5" loaf pan or several undivided ice trays. Cover with foil or plastic wrap. Place in freezer; freeze until firm, 3 to 6 hours. Stir 2 or 3 times with a fork or spoon while freezing. Makes about 4-1/2 cups.

Avocado Frozen Yogurt

Ever so smooth and creamy.

4 small or 2 large ripe avocados, peeled
1/4 cup lemon juice
2 cups orange juice

1-1/2 cups sugar
2 cups plain yogurt
1 teaspoon grated orange peel

In blender or food processor, puree avocado, lemon juice, orange juice and sugar; set aside. In a large bowl, stir yogurt until smooth. Stir in avocado mixture and orange peel. Pour into ice cream canister. Freeze in ice cream maker according to manufacturer's directions. **Freezer method:** Pour prepared mixture into a 9-inch square pan or several undivided ice trays. Cover with foil or plastic wrap. Place in freezer; freeze until firm, 3 to 6 hours. Stir 2 or 3 times with fork or spoon while freezing. For a smoother texture, freeze until almost firm, 1 to 3 hours. Break into small pieces. Spoon half of mixture into a chilled large bowl or chilled food processor bowl. Beat with electric mixer or metal food processor blade until light and fluffy but not thawed. Repeat with remaining partially frozen mixture. Return beaten mixture to pan and freeze until firm, 1 to 3 hours. Makes about 2 quarts.

Melons & Vegetables

If you've not yet been converted to these wonderful fresh melon flavors, you'll never be able to resist the heavenly color and appealing flavor of Watermelon Ice. It is almost 100% fresh watermelon. The fruit is pureed until it is almost liquid but still has tiny pieces of fruit in it. High water content makes melons quick and easy to puree. Add light corn syrup, sugar and some lemon juice and it's ready to be frozen.

If you own an ice cream maker, use it to freeze any of the fruit mixtures. Or pour mixtures into 9-inch square baking pans or loaf pans and freeze them in your freezer. With a fork or spoon, stir the mixture two or three times during freezing and you'll end up with a refreshing icy texture. If you want a superb, light dessert, beat the frozen mixture in a food processor with the metal blade until fluffy. You'll find it hard to believe it's the same mixture. Work quickly so it doesn't melt, then serve immediately or freeze it until firm.

Cantaloupe, honeydew and crenshaw melon colors are not as dramatic as watermelon, but their fresh melon flavors are wonderful. Buy melons that are fairly firm, not soft. They can be held several days in a warm place out of direct sunlight but, if they begin to soften, use them immediately.

Have you considered vegetable frozen desserts and first courses? Golden Glow Yogurt might be just the solution to getting your youngsters to eat carrots. Green Chowder Frappé has a subtle flavor even the most discriminating person will have trouble identifying. And Gazpacho Frappé is guaranteed to be a conversation starter at your next VIP dinner party. Serve either the frappé or freeze in your most elegant wine or sherbet glasses. Furnish guests with spoons, but expect them to drink the slowly thawing mixture.

Cantaloupe Sherbet   Photo at left.

Perfect ending to a backyard barbecue.

1 medium cantaloupe	1/4 cup honey
2 tablespoons lemon juice	3 cups half-and-half
1/2 cup sugar	1/2 teaspoon vanilla extract

Cut cantaloupe from rind; remove and discard seeds. Cut fruit into 1-inch cubes. Puree cantaloupe cubes and lemon juice in blender or food processor until almost smooth. In a large bowl, combine sugar, honey and half-and-half. Add pureed cantaloupe mixture and vanilla. Stir until sugar dissolves. Pour into ice cream canister. Freeze in ice cream maker according to manufacturer's directions. **Freezer method:** Pour prepared mixture into a 9-inch square pan or several undivided ice trays. Cover with foil or plastic wrap. Place in freezer; freeze until firm, 3 to 6 hours. Stir 2 or 3 times with a fork or spoon while freezing. For a smoother texture, freeze prepared mixture until almost firm, 1 to 3 hours. Break into small pieces. Spoon half of mixture into a chilled large bowl or chilled food processor bowl. Beat with electric mixer or metal food processor blade until light and fluffy but not thawed. Repeat with remaining frozen mixture. Return beaten mixture to pan and freeze until firm, 1 to 3 hours. Makes about 2 quarts.

Cantaloupe-Wine Sorbet

Vary this recipe with your favorite wine.

1/2 cup sugar	1 large ripe cantaloupe
1/4 cup light corn syrup	1 tablespoon lemon juice
3/4 cup water	1 cup sauterne wine

In a small saucepan, combine sugar, corn syrup and water. Stir over low heat until sugar dissolves; cool to room temperature. Cut cantaloupe from rind; remove and discard seeds. Cut fruit into 1-inch cubes. Puree cantaloupe cubes and lemon juice in blender or food processor until smooth. In a medium bowl, combine puree, cooled syrup and wine. Pour into ice cream canister. Freeze in ice cream maker according to manufacturer's directions. **Freezer method:** Pour prepared mixture into a 9-inch square pan or several undivided ice trays. Cover with foil or plastic wrap. Place in freezer; freeze until firm, 3 to 6 hours. Scrape frozen mixture with a fork or spoon until pieces resemble finely crushed ice. Serve immediately. For a smoother texture, freeze prepared mixture until firm; break into small pieces. Spoon half of frozen mixture into chilled food processor bowl. Beat with metal blade until light and fluffy but not thawed. Repeat with remaining frozen mixture. Serve immediately or return beaten mixture to pan and freeze until firm, 1 to 3 hours. Makes about 2 quarts.

Medley of: Sicilian Melon Ice made with Honeydew Melon, page 97, Cantalope Sherbet, above, and Watermelon Sorbet, page 97.

Cantaloupe Ice

An excellent brunch finale.

1 medium cantaloupe, peeled	**1/3 cup honey**
2 tablespoons lemon juice	**1/8 teaspoon salt**

Remove and discard cantaloupe seeds. Cut fruit into cubes. Combine in blender or food processor with lemon juice, honey and salt. Puree until almost smooth. Pour into a 9" x 5" loaf pan or several undivided ice trays. Cover with foil or plastic wrap. Place in freezer; freeze until firm, 3 to 6 hours. Stir 2 or 3 times while freezing. For a smoother texture, freeze prepared mixture until firm. Break frozen mixture into small pieces. Spoon into chilled food processor bowl. Beat with metal blade until light and fluffy but not thawed. Serve immediately or return beaten mixture to pan; freeze until firm, 1 to 3 hours. Makes about 1 quart.

Crenshaw Ice Cream

Challenge your guests to identify this flavor.

1/2 crenshaw melon, peeled	**1 cup whipping cream**
2 cups half-and-half	**1/2 teaspoon vanilla extract**
3/4 cup sugar	**1 tablespoon lemon juice**
4 egg yolks, well beaten	

Remove melon seeds. Cut fruit into cubes. Puree in blender or food processor until smooth; set aside. In a medium saucepan, combine half-and-half, sugar and beaten egg yolks. Cook and stir over low heat until mixture is slightly thickened and coats a metal spoon. Stir in pureed melon, whipping cream, vanilla and lemon juice. Cool to room temperature. Pour into canister. Freeze in ice cream maker according to manufacturer's directions. Makes 2 quarts.

Watermelon Ice

Tastes just like fresh, ice-cold watermelon.

1/4 medium watermelon	**1/3 cup sugar**
1/3 cup light corn syrup	**1 tablespoon lemon juice**

Cut melon from rind, reserving only red fruit. Remove and discard seeds. Cut fruit into 1-inch cubes. Puree watermelon cubes half at a time in blender or food processor. In a medium bowl, combine pureed watermelon, corn syrup, sugar and lemon juice. Pour into ice cream canister. Freeze in ice cream maker according to manufacturer's directions. **Freezer method:** Pour prepared mixture into a 9-inch square pan or several undivided ice trays. Cover with foil or plastic wrap. Place in freezer; freeze until firm, 3 to 6 hours. Scrape frozen mixture with a fork until pieces resemble finely crushed ice. For a smoother texture, freeze prepared mixture until firm; break into small pieces. Spoon half of mixture into chilled food processor bowl. Beat with metal blade until light and fluffy but not thawed. Repeat with remaining frozen mixture. Serve immediately or return beaten mixture to pan and freeze until firm, 1 to 3 hours. Makes about 2 quarts.

Sicilian Melon Ice   *Photo on page 94.*

Midsummer blue-ribbon winner.

1-1/2 cups sugar
1-1/2 cups water

1 medium honeydew or crenshaw melon
2 teaspoons lime juice

In a medium saucepan, combine sugar and water. Stir over medium heat until sugar dissolves. Stirring occasionally, cook to 234°F (112°C) on a candy thermometer or until syrup spins a 2-inch thread when slowly poured from a spoon. Set aside to cool at room temperature 10 minutes. Cut melon from rind; remove and discard seeds. Cut fruit into 1-inch cubes. Puree melon cubes and lime juice in blender or food processor until almost smooth. Stir puree into reserved syrup. Pour into ice cream canister. Freeze in ice cream maker according to manufacturer's directions. **Freezer method:** Pour prepared mixture into a 9-inch square pan or several undivided ice trays. Cover with foil or plastic wrap. Place in freezer; freeze until firm, 3 to 6 hours. Scrape frozen mixture with a fork until pieces resemble finely crushed ice. For a smoother texture, freeze prepared mixture until firm; break into small pieces. Spoon half of mixture into chilled food processor bowl. Beat with metal blade until light and fluffy but not thawed. Repeat with remaining frozen mixture. Serve immediately or return beaten mixture to pan and freeze until firm, 1 to 3 hours. Makes about 2 quarts.

Watermelon Sorbet   *Photo on page 94.*

Lovely to look at and delightful to eat.

2/3 cup sugar
1/2 cup water
2/3 cup light corn syrup

2 tablespoons lemon juice
1/4 large watermelon

In a medium saucepan, combine sugar, water and corn syrup. Stir over medium heat until mixture comes to a boil. Without stirring, simmer over low heat 5 minutes. Stir in lemon juice; cool to room temperature. Cut melon from rind, reserving only red fruit. Remove and discard seeds. Cut fruit into 1-inch cubes, making about 8 cups. Puree melon cubes about 2 cups at a time in blender or food processor. Stir into cooled syrup. Pour into ice cream canister. Freeze in ice cream freezer according to manufacturer's directions. **Freezer method:** Pour prepared mixture into a 9-inch square pan or several undivided ice trays. Cover with foil or plastic wrap. Place in freezer; freeze until firm, 3 to 6 hours. Scrape frozen mixture with a fork until pieces resemble finely crushed ice. For a smoother texture, freeze prepared mixture until firm; break into small pieces. Spoon half of mixture into chilled food processor bowl. Beat with metal blade until light and fluffy but not thawed. Repeat with remaining frozen mixture. Serve immediately or return beaten mixture to pan and freeze until firm. Makes about 2 quarts.

Watermelon-Wine Cooler

Serve this lovely and refreshing dessert after a rich meal.

1/4 medium watermelon
1/2 cup sugar

1/3 cup light corn syrup
1/4 cup port wine

Cut melon from rind, reserving only red fruit. Remove and discard seeds. Cut fruit into 1-inch cubes. Puree melon cubes half at a time in blender or food processor. Pour into a medium bowl; set aside. In a small saucepan, combine sugar, corn syrup and wine. Stir over low heat until sugar dissolves; cool to room temperature. Stir into pureed watermelon. Pour into ice cream canister. Freeze in ice cream maker according to manufacturer's directions. **Freezer method:** Pour prepared mixture into a 9'' x 5'' loaf pan or several undivided ice trays. Cover with foil or plastic wrap. Place in freezer; freeze until firm, 3 to 6 hours. Scrape frozen mixture with a fork until pieces resemble finely crushed ice. Serve immediately or return scraped mixture to pan and freeze until firm, 1 to 3 hours. For a smoother texture, freeze prepared mixture until firm, 3 to 6 hours. Break into small pieces. Spoon half into chilled food processor bowl. Beat with metal blade until light and fluffy but not thawed. Repeat with remaining frozen mixture. Serve immediately or return beaten mixture to pan and freeze until firm, 1 to 3 hours. Makes about 6 cups.

How to Make Gazpacho Frappé

1/Cut green pepper in half. Remove core and seeds; cut into pieces before blending.

2/Scrape frozen mixture with a fork until pieces resemble finely crushed ice. Spoon into glasses.

Golden Glow Yogurt

Nutritious ingredients that kids really go for.

2 cups plain yogurt
2 cups orange juice
1/2 cup honey
1/2 cup sugar

4 medium carrots, grated (2 cups)
2 teaspoons grated orange peel
1/4 cup finely chopped raisins

In a medium bowl, stir yogurt until smooth. Add orange juice, honey and sugar. Stir until sugar dissolves. Stir in carrots, orange peel and raisins. Pour into ice cream canister. Freeze in ice cream maker according to manufacturer's directions. Stir frozen mixture to blend carrots and raisins before serving or storing. **Freezer method:** Pour prepared mixture into a 9-inch square pan or several undivided ice trays. Cover with foil or plastic wrap. Place in freezer; freeze until firm, 3 to 6 hours. Stir 2 or 3 times with a fork or spoon while freezing. Makes about 2 quarts.

Gazpacho Frappé

Serve this savory frappé as the first course of a Mexican dinner.

4 green onions
1 medium cucumber, peeled, cubed
1/2 green pepper, coarsely chopped
4 ripe tomatoes, coarsely chopped
1/2 teaspoon salt

1/4 teaspoon garlic salt
1/8 teaspoon paprika
1/8 teaspoon black pepper
1 cup beef broth or bouillon

Cut green onions into 1/2-inch lengths. In blender or food processor, combine green onion pieces, cucumber, green pepper and tomatoes. Blend until mixture is in very small pieces. In a large bowl, combine pureed mixture, salt, garlic salt, paprika, black pepper and broth or bouillon. Pour into a 9" x 5" loaf pan or several undivided ice trays. Cover with foil or plastic wrap. Place in freezer; freeze until firm, 3 to 6 hours. Scrape with a fork until pieces resemble finely crushed ice. Spoon into sherbet glasses or champagne glasses. Serve immediately. Makes 6 servings.

Pumpkin Ice Cream

Tastes like pumpkin pie with whipped cream.

1 (16-oz.) can pumpkin
1 cup packed brown sugar
1/4 teaspoon ground cinnamon
1/8 teaspoon ground nutmeg
1/4 teaspoon ground ginger

1 cup half-and-half
1/2 teaspoon grated orange peel
1/4 cup orange juice
2 cups whipping cream

In a large bowl, combine all ingredients, stirring to distribute evenly. Pour into ice cream canister. Freeze in ice cream maker according to manufacturer's directions. Makes about 2 quarts.

Frozen Rhubarb Custard

Mild rhubarb taste lets the custard flavor come through.

1/2 lb. fresh rhubarb,
   cut in 1-inch pieces (about 2 cups)
1/4 cup water
2 cups half-and-half
3 eggs, beaten

1-1/4 cups sugar
1 cup whipping cream
1 teaspoon grated orange peel
3 to 5 drops red food coloring

In a medium saucepan, combine rhubarb and water; cover and simmer until tender, 5 to 10 minutes. Puree in blender or food processor; set aside. In a medium saucepan, combine half-and-half, eggs and sugar. Cook and stir over low heat until mixture thickens and coats a metal spoon. Stir in pureed rhubarb, whipping cream, orange peel and food coloring. Pour into canister. Freeze in ice cream maker according to manufacturer's directions. Makes about 6 cups.

Green Chowder Frappé

Perfect first course dish when you entertain a VIP on a hot summer evening.

3 green onions, chopped
1/2 cup watercress leaves
1 cup fresh or frozen peas
2 cups chicken broth or bouillon
1 potato, peeled, chopped

1/2 teaspoon salt
1/8 teaspoon pepper
1/4 teaspoon seasoned salt
1/2 cup dairy sour cream
Sour cream for garnish

In a large saucepan, combine green onions, watercress, peas, broth or bouillon, potato, salt, pepper and seasoned salt. Bring to a boil over medium heat. Cover and simmer over low heat until vegetables are tender. Pour into blender or food processor. Puree until smooth. Pour into a large bowl; cool to room temperature. Stir in sour cream. Pour into a 9'' x 5'' loaf pan or several undivided ice trays. Cover with foil or plastic wrap. Place in freezer; freeze until slushy, 1 to 3 hours. Spoon into sherbet glasses or champagne glasses. Garnish top with sour cream. Serve immediately. If mixture freezes solid, scrape with a fork until pieces resemble finely crushed ice. Serve immediately. Makes 4 to 6 servings.

Pies & Cakes

Pies and cakes are symbols of hospitality. They are served as special occasion dinner desserts and when friends drop in for the evening. Frozen pies have an advantage over non-frozen pies. If kept frozen, they can be made the day before without fear of a soggy crust or weeping meringue. Cookie crumb crusts are more compatible with frozen desserts and easier to handle than traditional pastry crusts. There's a wide variety of crumb flavors from which to choose. Vanilla wafers are mild-flavored and combine well with creamy-orange Harvey Wallbanger Pie. Chocolate cookies blend well with the coffee and chocolate flavors in Acapulco Mocha Pie and the mint and chocolate flavors in Chocolate-Mint Meringue Pie. Gingersnaps immediately came to mind for Frozen Eggnog-Pumpkin Pie. They contrast with the eggnog and the ginger goes well with the pumpkin mixture. Crushed pretzels are not usually used for pie crusts, but add a salty contrast in Margarita Pie.

Baked Alaska and Meringue Shells are not exactly pies, but have similar ingredients and uses. Baked Alaska and Aloha Baked Alaska are spectacular desserts designed to make an impression on your guests. They are not difficult to make but it's important to follow directions.

Ice Cream Roll and Gingerbread Roll are two more outstanding desserts that look impressive but aren't hard to make. Bake the cakes early enough to have them completely cooled, then fill with soft, spreadable ice cream. Use your own homemade ice cream or your favorite commercial brand.

Acapulco Mocha Pie

Have the fudge topping at room temperature for ease in spreading over the pie.

**35 chocolate cookies,
  crushed (1-1/2 cups)**
3 tablespoons butter, melted
1 pt. coffee ice cream, slightly softened

**1/2 cup chocolate fudge ice cream topping,
  room temperature**
1 cup whipping cream
2 tablespoons coffee liqueur

In a small bowl, combine cookie crumbs and butter. Reserve 1/4 cup crumb mixture. Press remaining crumb mixture over bottom and up side of a 9-inch pie plate. Refrigerate about 30 minutes. Spread softened ice cream over chilled crust. Spoon fudge topping evenly over ice cream. Cover with foil or plastic wrap. Place in freezer; freeze until firm, about 3 hours. In a small bowl, whip cream until soft peaks form. Gradually beat in liqueur until blended. Spread evenly over top of frozen pie. Sprinkle with reserved cookie crumbs. Cut into wedges; serve immediately or return completed pie to freezer until served. Makes 6 servings.

How to Make Margarita Pie

1/With back of a spoon, press crust mixture over bottom and up side of a 9-inch pie plate. Place in refrigerator 30 to 45 minutes.

2/Refrigerate custard mixture until it mounds when dropped from a spoon. Fold in beaten eggs. Spoon evenly into chilled pie shell.

Frozen Eggnog-Pumpkin Pie   *Photo on page 108.*

Perfect make-ahead dessert for holiday entertaining.

20 gingersnaps, crushed (1-1/2 cups)
2 tablespoons butter or margarine, melted
1 pt. eggnog ice cream or
    vanilla ice cream, softened
1 cup cooked pumpkin
3/4 cup sugar

1/2 teaspoon ground cinnamon
1/4 teaspoon ground nutmeg
1 tablespoon rum or brandy
1 cup whipping cream
Whipped cream for decoration, if desired

In a small bowl, combine gingersnap crumbs and butter or margarine. Press over bottom and up side of a 9-inch pie pan. Refrigerate at least 15 minutes. Spoon ice cream evenly over chilled crust. Smooth surface with back of a spoon. Cover with foil or plastic wrap. Place in freezer; freeze until firm, about 3 hours. In a medium bowl, combine pumpkin, sugar, cinnamon, nutmeg and rum or brandy; set aside. In a small bowl, whip 1 cup whipping cream until soft peaks form. Fold into pumpkin mixture. Spread evenly over ice cream. Return to freezer; freeze until firm, about 4 hours. Decorate with additional whipped cream, if desired.

Margarita Pie

All the flavors of a real Margarita including salty crust and slightly sweet filling.

1 cup finely crushed pretzels
3 tablespoons sugar
1/4 cup butter, melted
2/3 cup sugar
1 (.25-oz.) envelope unflavored gelatin
1 cup milk
2 egg yolks, beaten

1/4 cup lime juice
1/4 cup tequila
2 tablespoons Triple Sec
1 cup whipping cream
2 egg whites
Lime slices for decoration, if desired

In a small bowl, combine pretzel crumbs, 3 tablespoons sugar and butter. Press over bottom and up side of a 9-inch pie pan; refrigerate. In a medium saucepan, combine 2/3 cup sugar and gelatin. Gradually stir in milk and beaten egg yolks. Cook and stir over low heat until slightly thickened and mixture coats a metal spoon. Cool to room temperature. Stir in lime juice, tequila and Triple Sec. In a small bowl, whip cream until soft peaks form. Fold into custard mixture. Refrigerate until mixture mounds when dropped from a spoon, 30 to 45 minutes. In a small bowl, beat egg whites until stiff but not dry. Fold into partially set custard mixture. Spoon evenly into chilled pie shell. Cover with foil or plastic wrap. Place in freezer; freeze until firm, 3 to 4 hours. Place in re-frigerator about 15 minutes before serving time. To serve, cut into wedges; decorate with lime slices, if desired. Makes 6 servings.

Harvey Wallbanger Pie

It will remind you of the famous orange juice and Galliano drink.

32 vanilla wafers, crushed (1-1/2 cups)
1/4 cup butter or margarine, melted
1/2 cup sugar
1 *teaspoon* unflavored gelatin
1/8 teaspoon salt
1 cup orange juice

2 egg yolks, beaten
1/4 cup Galliano
1 teaspoon grated orange peel
2 egg whites
1 cup whipping cream
2 tablespoons toasted flaked coconut

In a small bowl, combine wafer crumbs and butter or margarine. Press over bottom and up side of a 9-inch pie pan; refrigerate. In a medium saucepan, combine sugar, gelatin and salt. Stir in orange juice and beaten egg yolks. Cook and stir over low heat until mixture thickens slightly. Stir in Galliano and orange peel. Refrigerate until mixture mounds when dropped from a spoon, 45 to 60 minutes. In a small bowl, beat egg whites until stiff but not dry. Fold into chilled orange mixture. In a small bowl, whip cream until soft peaks form; fold into orange mixture. Spoon into chilled vanilla wafer crust. Cover with foil or plastic wrap. Place in freezer; freeze until firm, 1 to 3 hours. Place in refrigerator about 15 minutes before serving time. To serve, cut into wedges; sprinkle with coconut. Makes 6 servings.

Brownie Igloos

When time is short, buy brownies at the bakery or use a mix.

1/4 cup butter or margarine
2 (1-oz.) squares unsweetened chocolate
2 eggs
1 cup sugar
1/4 teaspoon salt
1/2 teaspoon vanilla extract
1/2 cup all-purpose flour

1/2 cup chopped walnuts
9 scoops vanilla, banana or
    peppermint ice cream
4 egg whites
1/4 teaspoon cream of tartar
1/2 cup sugar

In a small saucepan, combine butter or margarine and chocolate. Stir over low heat until melted; set aside to cool. Preheat oven to 350°F (175°C). In a medium bowl, beat eggs until light and foamy. Beat in 1 cup sugar until thick and creamy. Beat in salt and vanilla. Stir in cooled chocolate mixture, then stir in flour. Fold in walnuts. Pour into an ungreased 8-inch square pan. Bake until mixture is set, about 20 minutes. Cool on a rack. Cut into 9 equal squares. Arrange on a large baking sheet. Top each brownie with a scoop of ice cream. Place baking sheet with brownies and ice cream in freezer. Freeze until ice cream is very firm, 2 to 4 hours. At serving time, preheat oven to 450°F (230°C). Beat egg whites with cream of tartar until foamy. Gradually beat in 1/2 cup sugar until stiff and glossy. Quickly spoon meringue over top and sides of ice cream and brownies, covering completely. Bake in preheated oven until lightly browned, 3 to 4 minutes. Serve immediately. Makes 9 servings.

Chocolate-Mint Meringue Pie

Freeze the peppermint-cream filling until it's firm enough to cut, but not icy-hard.

2 egg whites
1/3 cup granulated sugar
1/4 teaspoon vanilla extract
1/3 cup finely crushed chocolate
   cookie crumbs

1/4 cup chopped walnuts
1 cup whipping cream
2 tablespoons powdered sugar
1/3 cup crushed peppermint candy
1 (1-oz) square semisweet chocolate, grated

Thoroughly grease bottom and side of a 9-inch pie pan; set aside. Preheat oven to 325°F (165°C). In a medium bowl, beat egg whites until soft peaks form. Gradually beat in granulated sugar until stiff glossy peaks form. Fold in vanilla, cookie crumbs and walnuts. Spread evenly over bottom and up side of prepared pan. Bake in preheated oven 25 to 30 minutes. Cool to room temperature. About 3 hours before serving, whip cream in a small bowl until soft peaks form. Fold in powdered sugar and peppermint candy. Spread over cooled baked meringue. Sprinkle with grated chocolate. Place in freezer; freeze until firm, about 3 hours. Makes 6 servings.

Chocolate Cloud

Long cooking at a low temperature assures a crunchy meringue shell.

3 egg whites, room temperature
1/4 teaspoon cream of tartar
3/4 cup sugar
1-1/2 cups whipping cream

3/4 cup chocolate syrup
1/2 teaspoon vanilla extract
1/2 cup whipping cream
Grated semisweet chocolate

Line a large baking sheet with brown paper. Draw a 9-inch circle on paper; set aside. Preheat oven to 275°F (135°C). In a small bowl, beat egg whites and cream of tartar until soft peaks form. Gradually beat in sugar until very thick and glossy. Spoon beaten egg white mixture onto circle on paper. With a spoon, spread over entire circle, making side slightly thicker than bottom. Bake in preheated oven 75 minutes or until dry. Turn off heat; leave meringue in oven with door closed 60 minutes longer. Cool on a rack on counter; remove from paper. At least 4 hours before serving, whip 1-1/2 cups whipping cream in a small bowl until soft peaks form. Gradually fold in chocolate syrup and vanilla. Spread evenly in cooled meringue shell. In same bowl, whip 1/2 cup whipping cream until soft peaks form. Spoon whipped cream onto chocolate filling as a decoration. Sprinkle top with grated chocolate. Cover with foil or plastic wrap. Place in freezer; freeze at least 4 hours or until very firm. To serve, cut into wedges. Makes 6 to 8 servings.

To beat egg whites successfully, let them come to room temperature. Beat them in a clean bowl with beaters free from any trace of grease or oil.

1/Spread half of ice cream evenly into each pineapple shell. Cover and freeze at least 4 hours or until ice cream is firm.

2/Arrange chilled pineapple over firm ice cream. Spread meringue over ice cream and pineapple pieces, sealing to pineapple shells.

How to Make Aloha Baked Alaska

Baked Alaska

Use one layer of your favorite layer cake mix or buy one unfrosted layer cake at the bakery.

**1 qt. chocolate, vanilla or strawberry
    ice cream, slightly softened**
**1 (9-inch) single layer chocolate or
    white cake**
4 egg whites, room temperature

1/2 teaspoon cream of tartar
1/2 cup sugar
**Chocolate sauce or Raspberry Topping,
    page 155, if desired**

Spread ice cream in an 8-inch, round cake pan. Cover with foil or plastic wrap. Place in freezer; freeze at least 2 hours or until firm. Place single cake layer on a large baking sheet; refrigerate until ice cream is firm. Unmold ice cream by quickly dipping pan in lukewarm water. Invert onto top of chilled cake. Cake will extend about 1/2-inch beyond edge of ice cream. Freeze cake and ice cream about 1/2 hour or until ice cream is firm. At serving time, preheat oven to 450°F (230°C). In a large bowl, beat egg whites and cream of tartar until soft peaks form. Gradually beat in sugar until stiff peaks form. Quickly spread meringue evenly over cake and ice cream, covering completely. Seal meringue to baking sheet. Bake in preheated oven until meringue is browned, 4 to 5 minutes. Serve immediately. To serve, cut into wedges; top with chocolate sauce or Raspberry Topping, if desired. Makes 8 servings.

Aloha Baked Alaska

Covering the pineapple leaves with foil keeps them from burning.

1 fresh ripe pineapple	1/3 cup half-and-half
1 qt. coconut ice cream or	1/2 teaspoon vanilla extract
banana ice cream	1/4 cup chopped macadamia nuts or pecans
1 cup lightly packed brown sugar	4 egg whites, room temperature
3/4 cup light corn syrup	1/4 teaspoon cream of tartar
2 tablespoons butter or margarine	1/2 cup granulated sugar

Cut unpeeled pineapple and leaves in half lengthwise. Scoop pineapple out of shells; reserve shells. Discard core; cover pineapple leaves with foil. Cut fruit into 3/4-inch pieces; refrigerate. Spread half of ice cream evenly into each pineapple shell. Cover with foil or plastic wrap. Place in freezer; freeze at least 4 hours or until ice cream is firm. In a small saucepan, combine brown sugar, corn syrup and butter or margarine. Stir over medium heat until sugar dissolves; cool to lukewarm. Stir in half-and-half, vanilla and nuts; set aside. Preheat oven to 450°F (230°C). In a large bowl, beat egg whites and cream of tartar until soft peaks form. Gradually beat in granulated sugar until very thick and glossy. Top ice cream filled pineapple shells with chilled pineapple pieces. Quickly spread meringue over ice cream and pineapple pieces in each shell. Seal to edges of pineapple shells. Make peaks in meringue by touching surface with back of a spoon, then quickly lifting spoon. Place meringue-topped pineapple halves on a large baking sheet. Bake in preheated oven until meringue is lightly browned, 3 to 4 minutes. Remove foil from pineapple leaves. Serve immediately with brown sugar sauce. Makes 8 to 10 servings.

Meringue Shells

Try coffee ice cream and fudge sauce or strawberry ice cream and raspberry sauce.

3 egg whites, room temperature	1 qt. ice cream, your choice
1/4 teaspoon cream of tartar	1 cup sundae topping, your choice
3/4 cup sugar	

Cover two baking sheets with brown paper. Draw four 3-inch circles on each piece of paper; set aside. Preheat oven to 275°F (135°C). In a small bowl, beat egg whites and cream of tartar until soft peaks form. Gradually beat in sugar until very thick and glossy. Spoon meringue evenly into circles. With back of a spoon, spread meringue over circles, making sides slightly thicker than centers. Bake in preheated oven until dry, about 60 minutes. Turn off heat; leave meringue in oven with door closed 60 minutes longer. Cool on a rack on counter; remove from paper. Fill with ice cream of your choice; top with sundae topping. Serve immediately or place in freezer until serving time. Makes 8 servings.

On following pages, clockwise from center top: In old fashioned mold: Orange-Honey Yogurt, page 51, Chocolate Chip Mint Ice Cream, page 26 and Lemon Sherbet, page 55; Gingerbread Roll, page 110; Frozen Eggnog-Pumpkin Pie, page 103.

Gingerbread Roll   *Photo on page 108.*

The aroma of gingerbread baking will remind you of Grandma's kitchen.

4 eggs	**1/2 teaspoon ground ginger**
1/2 cup sugar	**1/2 cup molasses**
3/4 cup all-purpose flour	**Powdered sugar**
1/2 teaspoon baking soda	**1 qt. lemon frozen yogurt,**
1/4 teaspoon salt	**orange frozen yogurt, or**
1/2 teaspoon ground cinnamon	**Apple-Walnut Custard, page 76,**
1/4 teaspoon ground allspice	**slightly softened**

Grease bottom and side of a 15-1/2'' x 10-1/2'' baking sheet with raised sides. Line bottom with waxed paper. Grease paper; set aside. Preheat oven to 375°F (190°C). In a large bowl, beat eggs until thick and lemon colored. Gradually beat in sugar until thick and smooth. Stir in flour, baking soda, salt, cinnamon, allspice and ginger. Stir in molasses; beat until smooth. Pour into prepared baking sheet. Bake in preheated oven 12 to 15 minutes or until cake shrinks from sides of pan. Lay a clean towel on a flat surface. Dust with powdered sugar. When cake is baked, immediately turn out onto prepared towel. Remove waxed paper. Carefully roll up warm cake and towel from narrow end of cake. When cool, carefully unroll cake and remove towel. Spread frozen yogurt or ice cream evenly over cake. Reroll cake and wrap in foil. Serve immediately or place in freezer until serving time. To serve, cut in slices. Makes about 10 slices.

Ice Cream Roll

In the summer, fill with fresh peach ice cream or fresh strawberry ice cream.

4 egg whites, room temperature	**2 tablespoons water**
1/4 teaspoon cream of tartar	**1/2 cup all-purpose flour**
1/3 cup granulated sugar	**Powdered sugar**
4 egg yolks	**1 qt. chocolate ice cream or**
1/3 cup granulated sugar	**Rocky Road Ice Cream, page 26**
1 teaspoon lemon juice	

Preheat oven to 350°F (175°C). Grease a 15-1/2'' x 10-1/2'' baking sheet with raised sides. Line with waxed paper; grease waxed paper. In a large bowl, beat egg whites and cream of tartar until soft peaks form. Gradually beat in 1/3 cup granulated sugar until peaks are stiff but not dry. In a medium bowl, beat egg yolks until thick and lemon colored. Gradually beat in 1/3 cup granulated sugar, lemon juice and water. Fold egg yolk mixture into beaten egg whites, then fold in flour. Spread evenly in prepared baking sheet. Bake 15 minutes or until cake springs back when touched in center with your finger. Lay a clean towel on a flat surface. Dust with powdered sugar. When cake is baked, immediately turn out onto prepared towel. Remove waxed paper. Carefully roll up warm cake and towel from narrow end of cake. When cool, carefully unroll cake and remove towel. Spread ice cream evenly over cake. Reroll cake and wrap in foil. Place in freezer; freeze at least 6 hours until very firm. To serve, cut in slices. Makes about 10 servings.

Frozen Lime Cheesecake

One of our favorite cheesecakes in frozen form.

15 pieces zwieback toast,	**1 cup sugar**
crushed (1-1/4 cups)	**1/4 cup lime juice**
1/4 cup butter or margarine, melted	**1/2 teaspoon grated lime peel**
2 tablespoons sugar	**3 egg whites**
1 cup cottage cheese	**Whipped cream for decoration, if desired**
1 cup dairy sour cream	**Grated lime peel for decoration, if desired**
3 egg yolks	

In a small bowl, combine zwieback crumbs, butter or margarine and 2 tablespoons sugar. Press over bottom and about 1-1/2 inches up side of an 8-inch springform pan. In blender or food processor, combine cottage cheese, sour cream, egg yolks, 1 cup sugar, lime juice and 1/2 teaspoon lime peel. Process until smooth. In a large bowl, beat egg whites until stiff but not dry. Gradually fold in cottage cheese mixture. Pour into crumb-lined pan. Cover with foil or plastic wrap. Place in freezer; freeze until firm, 3 to 6 hours. Remove side of pan. If desired, decoration top with whipped cream and sprinkle of grated lime peel. To serve, cut into wedges. Makes 8 to 10 servings.

Frozen Mocha Cheesecake

For variety, substitute chocolate cookie crumbs for zwieback crumbs.

24 pieces zwieback toast,	**3/4 cup sugar**
crushed (2 cups)	**2 (1-oz.) squares semisweet**
2 tablespoons sugar	**chocolate pieces, grated**
1/3 cup butter, melted	**1 tablespoon instant coffee powder**
3 egg yolks	**3 egg whites**
1 (8-oz.) pkg. cream cheese, softened	**1 cup whipping cream**

In a small bowl, combine zwieback crumbs, 2 tablespoons sugar and butter. Press over bottom and about 2 inches up side of a 9-inch springform pan; refrigerate. In a large bowl, beat egg yolks, cream cheese and 3/4 cup sugar until smooth and creamy. Stir in grated chocolate and coffee powder; set aside. In a medium bowl, beat egg whites until stiff but not dry. In a small bowl, whip cream until soft peaks form. Fold beaten egg whites and whipped cream into cream cheese mixture. Spoon into crumb-lined pan. Cover with foil or plastic wrap. Place in freezer; freeze until firm, 5 to 6 hours. Makes 8 to 10 servings.

Just for Kids

Once children taste ice cream, they are fans for life. It is as popular at birthday celebrations as the traditional birthday cake.

Delight your children and their birthday guests with Ice Cream Clowns. Make large round scoops of ice cream for the heads the day before the party. Keep them in the freezer so they will be frozen firm. At the same time, frost and decorate ice cream cones for hats. Store these in the refrigerator. When its time to serve refreshments, each clown is easily and quickly assembled.

Ice cream sandwiches are popular with teenagers as well as young children. They are much less expensive to make than to buy. And you make them with your child's favorite ice cream flavor. Make your own cookies or cakes or buy packaged cookies. Make several ice cream sandwiches at a time, keeping the rest of the ice cream in the freezer until it is needed. To prevent melted sandwiches, quickly slip each sandwich into a plastic sandwich bag. Or wrap in foil and place in the freezer. Freeze them an hour or two before they are served.

Children love all kinds of frozen pops. Use popsicle molds or 3- or 5-ounce paper cups. Paper cups are available in most grocery stores. Partially freeze the mixture until it is slushy before inserting the sticks, then they will remain upright. Continue to freeze until firm. At serving time, peel off the paper cups. The ice pop is held by the stick and eaten like an ice cream cone.

Of interest to children of all ages are the Ice Cream Bonbons. Actually, they are miniature balls of ice cream made with a melon baller, then coated with chocolate. We used vanilla ice cream for the centers but you could use coffee, chocolate, caramel or banana. Pick up the bonbons in your fingers and eat them like candy.

Ice Cream Clown

Serve one clown to each guest at your child's birthday party.

1 qt. vanilla ice cream or
   chocolate ice cream
8 raisins, cut in half
4 long red gumdrops,
   cut in half lengthwise
1/3 cup toasted coconut
2 tablespoons butter or margarine, melted
1 tablespoon unsweetened cocoa powder

1-1/2 tablespoons milk
1 cup sifted powdered sugar
8 ice cream cones
2 tablespoons multi-colored candy
   cake decors
8 (3-inch) chocolate chip cookies,
   oatmeal cookies or sugar cookies

Place a 15-1/2" x 12" baking sheet in freezer to chill, at least 10 minutes. Using a large ice cream scoop, make 8 large ice cream balls to be used as clown heads. Arrange on chilled baking sheet. Working quickly, place 2 raisin halves on each ball to represent eyes. Place a slightly curved piece of gumdrop below the eyes to represent the mouth. Sprinkle toasted coconut over top of each ice cream ball to represent hair. Immediately place baking sheet with ice cream clown heads in freezer. Freeze until firm, about 3 hours. In a small bowl, combine melted butter or margarine, cocoa powder, milk and powdered sugar; beat until smooth. Spread a thin layer of frosting on outside of each ice cream cone; sprinkle with cake decors. Refrigerate until frosting sets. At serving time, arrange 8 small plates on a flat surface. Place one cookie in center of each plate; top each cookie with a frozen clown's head. Place a frosted cone, upside down, on each head. Serve immediately. Makes 8 servings.

Chocolate Ice Cream Sandwiches

You'll need a brick-shaped carton of ice cream to make these sandwiches.

2 cups flour
1 teaspoon baking soda
1/4 teaspoon salt
1/4 cup unsweetened cocoa powder
1 cup sugar
1 egg

1/3 cup vegetable oil
1 teaspoon vanilla extract
3/4 cup milk
1/2 gallon vanilla ice cream or chocolate
   ice cream in rectangular carton

Grease a 15-1/2" x 10-1/2" baking sheet with raised sides. Line with waxed paper. Grease waxed paper; set aside. Preheat oven to 350°F (175°C). In a large bowl, combine flour, baking soda, salt, cocoa powder and sugar. Make a well in center of mixture; add egg, oil, vanilla and milk. Beat until smooth. Spread evenly in prepared pan. Bake in preheated oven 12 minutes or until cake pulls away from sides of pan. Cool on a rack. Invert cooled cake onto a flat surface; remove pan. Remove waxed paper. Cut lengthwise into 3 equal pieces. Cut crosswise in 5 equal rows, making 15 individual cakes. Cut each individual cake in half horizontally; set aside. Remove and discard ice cream carton. Place ice cream broad-side down on a cutting board. Cut crosswise into 3 pieces, about 5" x 3-1/4" x 2-1/3" each. Cut each piece into five 1-inch slices. Place each ice cream slice between cut halves of each horizontally sliced individual cake. Place each sandwich in a small plastic bag or wrap in foil. Place in freezer; freeze until firm, 1 to 3 hours. Makes 15 sandwiches.

Peanut-Butter Graham-Cracker Sandwiches

An ideal make-ahead treat for your Scout Troop.

**64 individual graham crackers
(about 1 pound)
3/4 cup peanut butter**

**3/4 cup thick fudge ice cream topping
1/2 gallon chocolate ice cream in
rectangular carton**

Spread one side of 32 graham crackers with peanut butter; set aside. Spread one side of remaining graham crackers with fudge topping. Remove and discard carton from ice cream. Place ice cream broad-side down on a cutting board. Cut crosswise into eight 3/4-inch slices. Cut each slice in fourths. Sandwich one piece of ice cream between a fudge-coated and a peanut-butter-coated cracker. Place each sandwich in a small plastic bag or wrap each in foil. Place in freezer; freeze until firm, 1 to 3 hours. Makes 32 sandwiches.

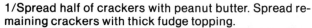

How to Make Peanut-Butter Graham-Cracker Sandwiches

1/Spread half of crackers with peanut butter. Spread remaining crackers with thick fudge topping.

2/Cut 1/2-gallon rectangular brick of ice cream into 8 slices. Cut each slice into quarters.

Frozen Bananas

These bananas are cut in half so small children can handle them more easily.

1/4 cup butter or margarine
1 (6-oz.) pkg. semisweet chocolate pieces
** (1 cup)**

3 tablespoons evaporated milk
5 or 6 bananas
1/3 cup finely chopped nuts, if desired

Line a large baking sheet with waxed paper; set aside. Combine butter or margarine and chocolate pieces in a small skillet. Stir over low heat until melted. Stir in evaporated milk; set aside. Peel bananas; cut each in half. Insert a wooden skewer into cut end of each banana half. Dip skewered bananas into hot chocolate mixture one at a time, turning to coat completely. If desired, dip into chopped nuts before chocolate sets. Arrange on prepared baking sheet. Place in freezer; freeze until firm, about 1 hour. Store frozen bananas in freezer bags or boxes or wrap airtight in foil. Remove from freezer 10 minutes before serving. Makes 10 to 12 servings.

3/Place ice cream slices on top of chocolate coated crackers. Top with crackers spread with peanut butter.

4/Immediately insert ice cream sandwiches into plastic sandwich bags. Return to freezer or serve immediately.

Ice Cream Cake

Substitute your favorite ice cream and sherbet flavors for the ones we used.

**1 qt. chocolate ice cream,
   slightly softened**
1 qt. orange sherbet, slightly softened
1 qt. vanilla ice cream

1 cup whipping cream
1 tablespoon powdered sugar
2 tablespoons unsweetened cocoa powder

Place two 8-inch, round cake pans in freezer to chill, about 10 minutes. Assemble a tall container of cold tap water, a long metal flexible-blade spatula and a damp sponge or 3 or 4 damp folded paper towels. As you work, occasionally dip spatula in water then dry with sponge or paper towels. This will keep ice cream from adhering to blade. **To make cake:** With spatula, spread chocolate ice cream evenly in one chilled cake pan. Cover with foil or plastic wrap; place in freezer. Spread orange sherbet in remaining chilled cake pan. Cover with foil or plastic wrap; place in freezer with chocolate ice cream. Freeze at least 1 hour or until firm. Place a 10- or 12-inch plate in freezer to chill. Spoon vanilla ice cream into a large bowl. Stir to soften; set aside. Working rapidly, remove cover and run tip of spatula around edge of frozen chocolate ice cream. Wipe bottom of pan with a warm, damp cloth to loosen ice cream. Invert onto chilled plate; remove pan. Spread 1/4-inch softened vanilla ice cream over top of chocolate layer; set aside. Remove cover and run tip of spatula around edge of frozen orange sherbet. Wipe bottom of pan with a warm damp cloth to loosen sherbet. Invert onto top of vanilla layer; remove pan. Spread 1/4-inch softened vanilla ice cream over top of orange layer. Spread remaining softened vanilla ice cream over side of ice cream cake. Place frosted cake in freezer 1 hour or until firm. In a small bowl, whip cream until soft peaks form. Gradually beat in powdered sugar and cocoa powder until stiff. Spoon whipped cream mixture into a pastry bag; decorate frozen cake. Return to freezer at least 15 minutes before serving. To serve, cut into wedges, dipping knife in cold water after each cut. Makes 12 to 16 servings.

Ice Cream Bonbons

For a chocolate-pecan flavor combination, try this recipe with butter-pecan ice cream.

1 pt. vanilla ice cream
1/4 cup butter or margarine

1 (6-oz.) pkg. semisweet chocolate pieces
3 tablespoons evaporated milk

Line a large baking sheet with foil or waxed paper. Place in freezer to chill at least 10 minutes. Working quickly, use large melon baller to scoop small balls of ice cream. Arrange ice cream balls on chilled, lined baking sheet. Place in freezer; freeze at least 2 hours or until very firm. In a small saucepan, combine butter or margarine and chocolate pieces. Stir over low heat until melted. Stir in evaporated milk. Cool to room temperature. Working quickly, use a fork to lift frozen balls of ice cream one at a time and dip into cooled chocolate mixture. Quickly turn with fork to coat evenly. Lift from sauce with fork and arrange on baking sheet. Repeat dipping until all bonbons have been coated. Return to freezer; freeze until serving time. Makes 30 to 35 bonbons.

Birthday Cake with Orange Cream Sherbet, page 52, Old-Fashioned Vanilla Ice Cream, page 20 and Old-Fashioned Chocolate Ice Cream, page 25.

Easy Fruit Pops

Popular snack on hot afternoons.

**1 (10-oz.) pkg. frozen strawberries,
partially thawed**
1 cup water

**1/2 (6.2-oz.) envelope sweetened
strawberry-flavored drink mix
(1/2 cup)**

Puree strawberries in blender or food processor until almost smooth. Add water and drink mix. Process 3 to 5 seconds or until blended. Pour evenly into 3-ounce paper cups or popsicle molds. Cover with foil or plastic wrap. Place in freezer; freeze until slushy, about 1 hour. Insert popsicle stick in center of each cup; freeze until firm, 1 to 3 hours. To serve, peel off paper. Makes 8 pops.

Fruit Salad Pops

You'll need 5-ounce paper cups and popsicle sticks for these kid-pleasers.

1 pt. orange or peach yogurt
1 (8-oz.) can fruit cocktail, well drained

In a small bowl, stir yogurt until smooth. Stir in fruit cocktail. Spoon mixture evenly into 5-ounce paper cups. Insert popsicle stick into center of each cup; freeze until firm, 1 to 3 hours. To serve, peel off paper. Serve immediately. Makes 5 pops.

*When preparing popsicles for children, make smaller
ones in 3-ounce cups and larger ones in 5-ounce cups.*

Grape-Yogurt Pops

Keep on hand for after-school snacks.

1 cup grape juice
1 (3-oz.) pkg. grape-flavored gelatin

1/4 cup light corn syrup
2 cups plain yogurt

In a small saucepan, combine grape juice, gelatin and corn syrup. Stir over low heat until gelatin dissolves; set aside. In a medium bowl, stir yogurt until smooth. Slowly stir in grape mixture. Pour into popsicle molds or 3-ounce paper cups. Cover with foil or plastic wrap. Place in freezer; freeze until slushy, about 1 hour. Insert popsicle stick in center of each cup; freeze until firm, 1 to 3 hours. To serve, peel off paper. Makes 10 to 12 pops.

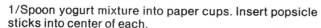

How to Make Fruit Salad Pops

1/Spoon yogurt mixture into paper cups. Insert popsicle sticks into center of each.

2/When frozen solid, peel off paper; serve immediately. The stick makes eating easier.

Rocky Road Cereal Ring

For youngsters of all ages.

4 cups crisp rice cereal	1 cup miniature marshmallows
1/4 cup butter or margarine	1/2 teaspoon vanilla extract
1/4 cup chopped walnuts or almonds	1 qt. chocolate ice cream
2 tablespoons honey	2/3 cup chocolate sauce or fudge sauce

Butter a large bowl. Pour cereal into buttered bowl; set aside. In a small saucepan, melt butter or margarine. Stir in walnuts or almonds, honey, marshmallows and vanilla. Pour over cereal; stir until evenly distributed. Press into a 6-1/2 cup ring mold. Refrigerate until firm, 30 to 60 minutes. Run a spatula around side to loosen. Invert onto a medium serving plate; remove mold. Scoop ice cream and arrange in center of ring. Spoon chocolate sauce or fudge sauce over top of ice cream and ring. Cut ring into wedges and serve immediately with ice cream balls. Makes 8 servings.

Snowballs

Insert one small candle in top of each snowball for a birthday celebration.

1 qt. vanilla ice cream or cherry ice cream	8 mint sprigs
1 cup flaked coconut	4 candied cherries, halved
	Chocolate sauce, if desired

Place a 15"x 12" baking sheet in freezer to chill, at least 10 minutes. Using a large ice cream scoop, make 8 large ice cream balls. Arrange on chilled baking sheet. Immediately place baking sheet with ice cream balls in freezer. Freeze at least 1 hour or until firm. Spread coconut in a pie pan or on a large sheet of foil. Roll firmly frozen ice cream balls in coconut until evenly coated. Return to freezer; freeze until firm, 1 to 3 hours. To serve, top each snowball with a sprig of mint and a half cherry. Serve plain or with chocolate sauce, if desired. Makes 8 servings.

Nuts, Candies & Caramels

Nut-flavored ice creams are the aristocrats of frozen desserts. To celebrate a special event, add nuts until they are generously sprinkled throughout the ice cream. Although nuts are expensive, the elegance they suggest is worth the extra cost. Before you add nuts to ice cream, taste them to be sure they are fresh.

Hazelnut Ice Cream Italiano is an American version of a delightful ice cream from Italy. Heat the nuts in the oven. Place the hot nuts in a dish towel to protect your hands and rub the nuts together to remove the skins. We like the ice cream best when the nut mixture is poured through a strainer to remove any trace of skins before it's frozen. It's delicious with or without straining.

Add chopped nuts or candies before ice cream mixtures are frozen or when the ice cream begins to increase in volume and becomes slightly firm. When you remove the dasher, use a long-handled spoon to stir the nuts or candies through the frozen ice cream mixture.

The names *butterscotch* and *caramel* are often used interchangeably because the flavors are similar. Actually, brown sugar gives butterscotch its flavor while the caramel flavor is created by caramelizing granulated sugar. Although the sugar should not be burned, it is commonly called *burnt sugar* because the sugar dissolves into a golden brown liquid as it heats.

Perhaps the best known candy-flavored ice cream is peppermint. Peppermint Stick Ice Cream has a delightfully refreshing taste. It is the ideal hot weather ice cream, yet blends perfectly with a mid-winter holiday menu. If hard candy is used, leave it in the wrapper and use a mallet or the handle of a knife to break it into pieces.

Butter-Pecan Ice Cream

Fantastic flavor! Our favorite ice cream for chocolate sundaes.

2 tablespoons butter
1/2 cup coarsely chopped pecans
1 cup packed brown sugar
1/2 cup water

2 eggs
1 teaspoon vanilla extract
2 cups half-and-half
1 cup whipping cream

In a small skillet, melt butter. Add pecans. Stir over low heat until pecans are golden brown but not burned; set aside. In a medium saucepan, combine brown sugar and water. Stir over medium heat until sugar dissolves and mixture comes to a boil. Stirring occasionally, simmer gently 2 minutes; set aside. In a medium bowl, beat eggs until thick and lemon colored, about 5 minutes. Beating constantly, immediately pour hot brown sugar syrup in a thin stream over beaten egg yolks. Continue beating until cool and thick; set aside. Stir in vanilla, half-and-half, whipping cream and toasted pecans. Pour into ice cream canister. Freeze in ice cream freezer according to manufacturer's directions. Makes about 2 quarts.

Butterscotch-Pecan Ripple

Let the ice cream soften enough to swirl sauce through. Don't let it melt.

1/2 cup lightly packed brown sugar
2 tablespoons light corn syrup
1/4 cup milk
1 tablespoon butter or margarine

1/4 cup finely chopped pecans
1/4 teaspoon vanilla extract
1/2 gallon vanilla ice cream,
   slightly softened

Place a 9-inch square pan in freezer to chill. In a small saucepan, combine brown sugar, corn syrup and milk. Cook and stir over medium heat until slightly thickened, 7 or 8 minutes. Stir in butter or margarine, pecans and vanilla. Cool to room temperature. Spoon softened ice cream into chilled 9-inch square pan. Pour cooled sauce in ribbons across top of ice cream. Pull a metal spatula back and forth evenly through ice cream to give a marbled effect. Cover with plastic wrap or foil. Place in freezer; freeze at least one hour or until firm, 3 to 6 hours. Makes 2 quarts.

Butterscotch Peanut-Butter Ice Cream

Butterscotch pieces can be found on the supermarket shelf next to chocolate pieces.

1 (6-oz.) pkg. butterscotch pieces (1 cup)
1/4 cup lightly packed brown sugar
1/4 cup chunky peanut butter

2 cups milk
1 teaspoon vanilla extract
2 cups half-and-half

In a medium saucepan, combine butterscotch pieces, brown sugar, peanut butter and milk. Stir over low heat until butterscotch pieces melt; cool to room temperature. Stir in vanilla and half-and-half. Pour into ice cream canister. Freeze in ice cream maker according to manufacturer's directions. Makes about 2 quarts.

Butterscotch Ice Cream

Add chopped pecans or almonds if you like nuts in your ice cream.

1 cup lightly packed dark brown sugar
1 tablespoon cornstarch
1/4 cup dark corn syrup
1/4 teaspoon salt
3 cups whole milk

2 eggs
1 (5.33-oz.) can evaporated milk
1 cup whipping cream
1 teaspoon vanilla extract

In a medium saucepan, combine brown sugar and cornstarch. Stir in corn syrup, salt and whole milk. Stir over medium heat until brown sugar melts and mixture begins to simmer; set aside. In a small bowl, beat eggs until blended. Stir about 1 cup hot milk mixture into eggs. Stir egg mixture into remaining milk mixture. Cook and stir over low heat until slightly thickened, about 2 minutes. Stir in evaporated milk, whipping cream and vanilla. Cool to room temperature. Pour into ice cream canister. Freeze in ice cream maker according to manufacturer's directions. Makes about 2 quarts.

Butterscotch Pudding Ice Cream

You don't have to cook this quick ice cream.

2 eggs
1 cup lightly packed brown sugar
3 cups milk
**2 (3-3/4-oz.) pkgs. instant
   butterscotch pudding mix**

2 cups half-and-half
1 cup chopped pecans

In a large bowl, beat eggs until light and fluffy. Beat in brown sugar, milk, and pudding until smooth. Stir in half-and-half and pecans. Pour into ice cream canister. Freeze in ice cream maker according to manufacturer's directions. Makes about 2 quarts.

Ice cream mixtures containing small pieces of nuts can be frozen in an ice cream maker.
Stir in large pieces of nuts or candy when the dasher is removed from the frozen ice cream.

Hazelnut Ice Cream Italiano

Any of the skin left on the toasted nuts is strained off before freezing.

8 oz. hazelnuts (about 2 cups)
3 cups milk
1 cup sugar

4 egg yolks
2 cups whipping cream
1/2 teaspoon vanilla extract

Preheat oven to 400°F (205°C). Arrange hazelnuts over bottom of a shallow 13" x 9" baking pan. Bake in preheated oven about 6 minutes or until skins begin to crack. Pour hot baked nuts onto center of a clean towel. Fold end of towel over nuts; rub briskly to remove most of skins. In blender or food processor, blend nuts by turning on and off until pieces resemble fine dry breadcrumbs. In a medium saucepan, combine finely chopped nuts, milk and sugar. Stir over medium heat until sugar dissolves and mixture comes to a boil; set aside. Cover and cool to room temperature. Line a strainer with cheesecloth. Place over a medium bowl. Pour cooled milk mixture into lined strainer. With back of a spoon, press as much liquid as possible through strainer; set aside. Discard cheesecloth and contents. In a small bowl, beat egg yolks until thick and lemon colored, about 5 minutes. In a medium saucepan, combine beaten egg yolks and strained milk mixture. Cook and stir over low heat until mixture thickens and coats a metal spoon. Cool to room temperature. Stir in whipping cream and vanilla. Pour into ice cream canister. Freeze in ice cream maker according to manufacturer's directions. Makes about 2 quarts.

How to Make Hazelnut Ice Cream Italiano

1/Bake hazelnuts in preheated oven about 6 minutes or until skins begin to crack.

2/Pour hot nuts onto center of a clean towel. Fold end of towel over nuts; rub briskly to remove most of skins.

Mardi Gras Cream

With a consistency this creamy, you'll want to include it in every celebration.

1/4 cup chopped blanched almonds
2 eggs
1/2 cup packed brown sugar
1 cup milk
3 bananas

1/2 cup apricot jam
2 tablespoons lemon juice
2 tablespoons rum
1 cup whipping cream

In a small skillet, toast blanched almonds over low heat until golden brown, 5 to 7 minutes; set aside. In a large bowl, beat eggs until thick and lemon colored, about 5 minutes. Beat in brown sugar until blended. Stir in milk and toasted almonds. Cut bananas into chunks. In blender or food processor, puree banana chunks, apricot jam and lemon juice. Stir into egg mixture. Stir in rum and whipping cream. Pour into ice cream canister. Freeze in ice cream maker according to manufacturer's directions. Makes about 2 quarts.

3/Process in blender or food processor, turning on and off until nuts resemble fine dry breadcrumbs.

4/Pour cooled milk mixture into lined strainer. Use back of spoon to press as much liquid as possible through strainer.

Peppermint-Stick Ice Cream

Stir more crushed candy into the finished ice cream to get a stronger peppermint flavor.

2 egg yolks, beaten
1/2 cup sugar
1 cup milk

1 cup whipping cream
1/2 cup crushed peppermint stick candy

In a small saucepan, combine beaten egg yolks, sugar and milk. Cook and stir over low heat until mixture is slightly thickened and coats a metal spoon. Remove from heat. Stir in whipping cream and 1/4 cup crushed candy. Cool to room temperature. Pour into ice cream canister. Freeze in ice cream maker according to manufacturer's directions. When frozen, stir in remaining crushed candy. Makes about 1 quart.

Candied Orange-Pineapple Cream

Turn-of-the-century family favorite.

1 (10-oz.) pkg. candy orange slices
2 (8-oz.) cans crushed pineapple in
  fruit juice

2/3 cup light corn syrup
1 cup whipping cream
1-1/2 cups half-and-half

Cut candy orange slices into 1/4-inch cubes, making about 1-1/3 cups. In a small saucepan, combine diced orange slices, pineapple with juice and corn syrup. Stir occasionally over medium-low heat until diced candy begins to melt, about 2 minutes. Candy should not be completely melted. Pour into a large bowl. Set aside and cool to room temperature. Stir in whipping cream and half-and-half. Pour into ice cream canister. Freeze in ice cream maker according to manufacturer's directions. **Freezer method:** Pour prepared mixture into a 9" x 5" loaf pan or several undivided ice trays. Cover with foil or plastic wrap. Place in freezer; freeze until firm, 3 to 6 hours. Stir 2 or 3 times with a fork or spoon while freezing. Makes about 2 quarts.

Licorice-Stick Ice Cream

Reminiscent of childhood days.

4 egg yolks
1 cup sugar
2 cups whipping cream
2 cups half-and-half

1 (5-oz.) pkg. licorice sticks,
  cut in 1/4-inch pieces (1 cup)
1 cup milk

In a small bowl, beat egg yolks until thick and lemon colored, 4 or 5 minutes. In a heavy medium saucepan, combine beaten egg yolks, sugar, whipping cream and half-and-half. Cook and stir over low heat until mixture thickens slightly and coats a metal spoon; set aside. In blender or food processor, combine cut up licorice sticks and milk. Process until licorice pieces resemble grains of cooked rice. Stir into egg mixture. Cool to room temperature. Pour into ice cream canister. Freeze in ice cream maker according to manufacturer's directions. Makes about 2 quarts.

Peppermint Stick Ice Cream

Praline Cups

Lacy Southern-style cups to complement your favorite ice cream.

3 tablespoons butter or margarine, melted
1/4 cup lightly packed brown sugar
2 tablespoons light corn syrup
1/4 cup finely chopped pecans

1/3 cup all-purpose flour
1/8 teaspoon salt
6 scoops vanilla, caramel or
  pecan ice cream

Preheat oven to 375°F (190°C). Grease a large baking sheet; set aside. In a medium bowl, combine butter or margarine, brown sugar, corn syrup, pecans, flour and salt until just blended. Bake 2 cookies at a time on prepared baking sheet. Spoon 1 rounded tablespoonful dough about 3 inches from center top of baking sheet. Spoon another rounded tablespoonful dough about 3 inches from center bottom of baking sheet. Using back of spoon, flatten mounds to 3-inch circles. Bake in preheated oven until golden brown and lacy, 6 to 8 minutes. Cool on baking sheet about 1 minute or until edges are firm enough to lift with spatula. Invert 6 custard cups or coffee cups onto a flat surface. Immediately, place each cookie on an inverted cup to cool. Press edges of cookies down slightly to conform to shape of cup. Repeat with remaining dough. To serve, fill cooled cups with ice cream. Makes 6 servings.

How to Make Praline Cups

1/Flatten a rounded tablespoon of dough with back of a spoon to form a 3-inch circle. Place only 2 cookies on each baking sheet.

2/Cool baked cookies about one minute. Lift with spatula and place on inverted custard cups. Press gently, molding to cup shape.

Maple-Walnut Ice Cream

Rich, creamy New England flavor treat.

1 cup walnuts	**1-1/2 cups milk**
4 egg yolks, beaten	**1 teaspoon vanilla extract**
2 cups maple-flavored syrup	**2 cups whipping cream**

Preheat oven to 325°F (165°C). Arrange walnuts over bottom of a shallow 12'' x 7'' baking pan. Toast in preheated oven until golden brown, 5 to 7 minutes. Process toasted nuts in blender or food processor until finely chopped; set aside. In a medium saucepan, combine beaten egg yolks, maple syrup and milk. Cook and stir over low heat until slightly thickened. Stir in chopped nuts, vanilla and whipping cream. Cool to room temperature. Pour into ice cream canister. Freeze in ice cream maker according to manufacturer's directions. **Freezer method:** Pour prepared mixture into a 9-inch square pan or several undivided ice trays. Cover with foil or plastic wrap. Place in freezer; freeze until firm, 3 to 6 hours. Stir 2 or 3 times while freezing. For a smoother texture, freeze prepared mixture until firm; break into small pieces. Spoon half of mixture into a chilled large bowl or chilled food processor bowl. Beat with electric mixer or metal food processor blade until light and fluffy but not melted. Repeat with remaining frozen mixture. Immediately return beaten mixture to pan and freeze until firm, 1 to 3 hours. Makes about 2 quarts.

3/When thoroughly cooled, carefully place on dessert plates. Gently fill each with a large scoop of ice cream.

Frozen Bayou Crunch

Scrape coconut and pecans from the dasher and stir through the soft ice cream.

1/4 cup butter or margarine	**4 egg yolks, beaten**
1 (6 oz.) pkg. semisweet chocolate pieces	**1 teaspoon vanilla extract**
(1 cup)	**1/2 cup chopped pecans**
1 (13-oz.) can evaporated milk	**1/2 cup flaked coconut**
1 cup packed brown sugar	**2 cups half-and-half**

In a medium saucepan, combine butter or margarine, chocolate pieces, evaporated milk, brown sugar and beaten egg yolks. Cook and stir over low heat until chocolate and sugar dissolve and mixture thickens slightly. Beat with a whisk until smooth. Cool about 10 minutes. Stir in vanilla, pecans, coconut and half-and-half. Pour into ice cream canister. Freeze in ice cream maker according to manufacturer's directions. Makes about 2 quarts.

Caramel Ice Cream

Real old fashioned burnt-sugar ice cream made with caramelized sugar.

1-1/4 cups sugar	**4 egg yolks**
3/4 cup boiling water	**1 cup whipping cream**
3 cups half-and-half	**2 teaspoons vanilla extract**

In heavy medium saucepan, stir sugar over medium heat until dissolved. Melted sugar will be golden but not browned. Remove from heat. Stirring constantly, pour in boiling water all at once. Stir over medium heat until mixture is smooth and comes to a boil. Boil until mixture resembles corn syrup, 10 to 12 minutes. Remove from heat. Stir in half-and-half. Continue stirring until mixture returns to a boil. In a small bowl, beat egg yolks until blended. Stir about 1/2 cup hot mixture into beaten eggs. Stir egg mixture into remaining hot mixture. Stirring constantly, simmer until mixture thickens slightly, 2 to 3 minutes. If mixture is not smooth, pour through a fine strainer. Stir in whipping cream and vanilla. Cool to room temperature. Pour into ice cream canister. Freeze in ice cream maker according to manufacturer's directions. Makes about 6 cups.

Rapidly chill a custard-type mixture by placing the bowl or pan in a larger bowl of ice cubes. Stir occasionally.

Molded Frozen Desserts

Create your own ice cream shapes to fit the season of the year or theme of a dinner party. Will you bring one dramatic frozen beauty to the table, or will you prepare the molded frozen dessert in small individual molds? We prefer to line muffin cups with small fluted paper cups and freeze individual servings.

Molds are available in a variety of shapes from hearts and flowers to animals and fruits. Bowls or other containers from your kitchen can also be used. Metal bowls are especially nice because the mixture freezes faster in metal. Individual molds hold about 1/2-cup of ice cream and usually come in sets of six or eight. They vary in designs but often are shaped like hearts, miniature ring molds or small fluted brioche pans. Custard cups and tart pans are also fun to use. Larger square or rectangular metal ice cream molds are available in gourmet pan shops. Most of them have a geometric or floral design on the bottom. You can also mold frozen desserts in a Bundt cake pan, an angel food cake pan, a springform pan, loaf pans or round, single layer cake pans.

The ring mold is the most popular frozen dessert shape. It is attractive and makes an elegant display when unmolded and the center is filled with fresh fruits or a small bowl of sauce.

To unmold ice cream, quickly dip the mold into a large bowl of lukewarm water. Immediately invert the mold onto a chilled platter and remove the mold. If it needs further loosening, run a thin metal spatula down one side of the mold. Serve immediately or place the platter and molded dessert in the freezer until frozen solid.

Burnt-Almond Mousse

Enjoy this light and airy maple dessert topped with a crunch of almonds.

3/4 cup slivered almonds
4 egg yolks, beaten
3/4 cup maple syrup
3/4 cup sugar
1/2 teaspoon vanilla extract

2 cups whipping cream
Whipped cream for decoration, if desired
Toasted chopped almonds for decoration,
   if desired

Chop slivered almonds. In a medium skillet, occasionally stir almonds over low heat until golden; set aside to cool. In a small saucepan, combine beaten egg yolks and maple syrup. Cook and stir over low heat until thickened; set aside to cool. Generously butter a 13'' x 9'' baking pan; sprinkle with toasted almonds; set aside. In a heavy medium skillet, stir sugar over medium heat until liquified and a golden caramel color. Immediately pour caramelized sugar over almonds. Cool to room temperature. Break into very small pieces by striking with a mallet or handle of a heavy knife. In a large bowl, combine cooked egg yolk mixture, crumbled almond candy and vanilla; set aside. In a medium bowl, whip cream until soft peaks form. Fold into almond mixture. Spoon into a 6-1/2 cup ring mold or bombe mold. Cover with foil or plastic wrap. Place in freezer; freeze until firm, 3 to 6 hours. Place a medium platter or tray in freezer to chill, at least 30 minutes. To unmold, dip frozen mold quickly in and out of lukewarm water to depth of contents. Invert onto chilled platter or tray; remove mold. Decorate with additional whipped cream and almonds, if desired. Makes 6 to 8 servings.

Peanut Crunch Mold

Rich and Creamy!

3/4 cup sugar
1/4 cup water
5 egg yolks
1 cup crushed peanut brittle

1 teaspoon vanilla extract
2 cups whipping cream
Crushed peanut brittle for decoration
Fudge sauce or caramel sauce

In a small saucepan, combine sugar and water. Stir over medium heat until mixture comes to a boil. Continue boiling without stirring until mixture reaches 238°F (114°C) on a candy thermometer or syrup forms a soft ball when dropped into very cold water, 10 to 15 minutes. In a large bowl, beat egg yolks until thick and lemon colored, about 5 minutes. Beating constantly, immediately pour hot syrup in a thin stream over beaten egg yolks. Continue beating until mixture is lukewarm, about 5 minutes. Stir in 1 cup crushed peanut brittle and vanilla. In a medium bowl, whip cream until soft peaks form. Fold into egg yolk mixture. Pour into a 9-cup mold or bowl. Cover with foil or plastic wrap. Place in freezer; freeze until firm, 3 to 6 hours. Place a medium platter or tray in freezer to chill, about 30 minutes. To unmold, dip frozen mold quickly in and out of lukewarm water to depth of contents. Invert onto chilled platter or tray; remove mold. Decorate with crushed peanut brittle. Serve with fudge sauce or caramel sauce.

1/Cool carmelized sugar and almonds. Turn out onto a hard surface; with a mallet or heavy object, lightly tap mixture until crumbled.

2/To serve, quickly dip mold in and out of lukewarm water. Invert onto platter; gently remove mold.

How to Make Burnt-Almond Mousse

Apricot Cream Mold

This special flavor treat is made in your freezer.

1/2 lb. marshmallows
1/4 cup orange juice
8 ripe apricots
1 cup whipping cream

1/4 teaspoon almond extract
Whipped cream for decoration, if desired
Chopped pecans for decoration, if desired

In a heavy medium saucepan, combine marshmallows and orange juice. Stir over low heat until marshmallows melt; set aside. Remove and discard apricot pits. Puree apricots in blender or food processor until smooth. Stir into melted marshmallow mixture. In a small bowl, whip 1 cup cream until soft peaks form. Fold whipped cream and almond extract into melted marshmallow mixture. Spoon into a 4-cup mold. Cover with foil or plastic wrap. Place in freezer; freeze until firm, about 4 hours. Place a medium serving plate in freezer to chill, about 30 minutes. To unmold, dip frozen mold quickly in and out of lukewarm water to depth of contents. Invert onto chilled serving plate; remove mold. To serve, cut into 5 or 6 slices. Decorate each slice with additional whipped cream and chopped pecans, if desired.

Royal Velvet Mousse

Always a favorite with chocolate fans.

1 (1-oz.) square unsweetened chocolate	3/4 cup sugar
2 (1-oz.) squares semisweet chocolate	2 tablespoons water
1/2 cup butter	3 egg whites, room temperature
2 tablespoons coffee liqueur	1/4 teaspoon cream of tartar
3 egg yolks	1/2 cup whipping cream

In a heavy small saucepan, combine unsweetened chocolate, semisweet chocolate and butter. Stir over low heat until chocolate melts. Stir in liqueur; set aside. In a small bowl, beat egg yolks until thick and lemon colored, about 4 minutes. In a small saucepan, combine sugar and water. Stir over medium heat until mixture begins to boil. Beating constantly, immediately pour hot mixture in a thin stream over beaten egg yolks. Pour water 2 inches deep in a large saucepan; bring to a simmer over medium heat; remove from heat. Place bowl with egg yolk mixture in pan of very hot water. Beat egg yolk mixture over pan of hot water until doubled in volume, about 5 minutes. Remove bowl from hot water; beat another 5 minutes. Fold melted chocolate mixture into beaten egg yolk mixture; set aside. In a medium bowl, beat egg whites and cream of tartar until stiff but not dry. Fold beaten egg whites into chocolate mixture; set aside. In a small bowl, whip cream until soft peaks form. Fold into chocolate mixture. Spoon mixture into a 5- or 6-cup bowl or soufflé dish. Cover with foil or plastic wrap. Place in freezer; freeze until firm, 3 to 6 hours. Place mixture in refrigerator 15 minutes before serving. To serve, spoon into dessert dishes. Makes 6 to 8 servings.

Mincemeat Mousse

Grand finale for a holiday dinner party.

3 egg yolks	3 egg whites, room temperature
3/4 cup sugar	1/4 teaspoon cream of tartar
1/2 cup orange juice	1/2 cup whipping cream
1/2 cup mincemeat	Chopped walnuts for decoration, if desired
1 tablespoon rum or brandy, if desired	Whipped cream for decoration, if desired

In a large bowl, beat egg yolks until thick and lemon colored, 4 to 5 minutes; set aside. In a small saucepan, combine sugar and orange juice. Stir over medium heat until mixture comes to a boil. Beating constantly, immediately pour hot orange syrup over beaten egg yolks. Continue beating until mixture doubles in volume, about 5 minutes. Stir in mincemeat and rum or brandy if desired; set aside. In a medium bowl, beat egg whites and cream of tartar until peaks are stiff but not dry. Fold into egg yolk mixture; set aside. In a small bowl, whip 1/2 cup cream until soft peaks form. Fold into egg yolk mixture. Spoon into a 6-cup mold or soufflé dish. Cover with foil or plastic wrap. Place in freezer; freeze until firm, 3 to 6 hours. Place a medium platter or serving plate in freezer to chill, at least 30 minutes. To unmold, dip frozen mold quickly in and out of lukewarm water to depth of contents. Invert onto chilled platter or plate; remove mold. Decorate with chopped walnuts and additional whipped cream. Cut into wedges to serve. Makes 8 servings.

Italian Peach Mousse

Wonderful way to capture fresh peach flavor.

6 fresh ripe peaches, peeled
2 tablespoons lemon juice
1/3 cup water
1 cup sugar

4 egg whites
1/4 teaspoon almond extract
1 cup whipping cream

Remove and discard peach pits. Puree peaches and lemon juice in blender or food processor until almost smooth; set aside. In a small saucepan, combine water and sugar. Stir over medium heat until mixture comes to a boil. Cover and boil 1 minute. Uncover; continue boiling until mixture reaches 238°F (114°C) on a candy thermometer or forms a soft ball when dropped into very cold water, 10 to 15 minutes. In a medium bowl, beat egg whites with electric mixer until soft peaks form. Beating constantly, immediately pour hot syrup in a thin stream over beaten egg whites. Continue beating until cool and thick. Stir in almond extract; set aside. In a small bowl, whip cream until soft peaks form; set aside. Fold peach puree into beaten egg white mixture. Then fold in whipped cream. Spoon into an 8-cup mold or bowl. Cover with foil or plastic wrap. Place in freezer; freeze until firm, about 4 hours. Place a medium platter or tray in freezer to chill, about 30 minutes. To unmold, dip mold quickly in and out of lukewarm water to depth of contents. Invert onto chilled platter or tray; remove mold. Let rest in refrigerator about 10 minutes before cutting. To serve, cut into slices or wedges. Makes 6 to 8 servings.

Peach Bombe

Use fresh, drained canned or frozen peaches.

1 qt. vanilla ice cream or
** butter-pecan ice cream, softened**
4 ripe peaches, peeled
1/4 cup light corn syrup

2 tablespoons peach brandy
1 cup whipping cream
1/8 teaspoon almond extract
Whipped cream for decoration

Place an 8-cup bombe mold into freezer to chill, about 30 minutes. Working quickly, line chilled mold with softened ice cream. Cover with foil or plastic wrap. Place in freezer; freeze until firm, 1 to 3 hours. Remove and discard peach pits. Chop peaches into a medium bowl. Stir in corn syrup and brandy. Cover and refrigerate. In a small bowl, whip 1 cup cream until soft peaks form. Stir in almond extract. Fold into peach mixture. Spoon peach mixture into center of bombe. Cover with plastic wrap or foil; freeze until firm, about 6 hours. Place a medium platter or tray into freezer to chill, about 30 minutes. To unmold, dip mold quickly in and out of lukewarm water to depth of contents. Invert onto chilled platter or tray; remove mold. Decorate with additional whipped cream, if desired. To serve, slice crosswise, dipping knife in lukewarm water before making each slice. Makes 10 to 12 servings.

It takes 4 to 5 minutes of beating with an electric mixer for eggs to become thick and lemon colored.

Chocolate-Mint Truffle Mold

After one bite, this will be a favorite at your house.

10 whole ladyfingers, split horizontally
1 cup butter, room temperature
2 cups sifted powdered sugar
3 (1-oz.) squares unsweetened chocolate,
  melted

4 eggs
1/2 teaspoon peppermint extract
Whipped cream for decoration, if desired

In bottom of an 8-inch springform pan, arrange 10 ladyfinger halves cut side down like spokes of a wheel. Reserve remaining ladyfinger halves. In a large bowl, beat butter and powdered sugar until light and fluffy. Beat in melted chocolate. Add eggs one at a time, beating well after each addition. Stir in peppermint extract. Gently spoon into pan without disturbing ladyfingers in pan. Over top of filling, arrange reserved ladyfinger halves cut side down like spokes of a wheel. Cover pan with foil or plastic wrap. Place in freezer; freeze at least 4 hours. Remove side of pan; cut into wedges. Decorate with whipped cream, if desired. Makes 8 servings.

Neapolitan Cake Mold

An updated version of nostalgic Neapolitan ice cream.

1 qt. chocolate ice cream,
  slightly softened
1 pt. vanilla ice cream
1 pt. strawberry ice cream

1 cup whipping cream
1/4 cup toasted sliced almonds
Fresh strawberries for decoration

Place a 9-inch fluted tube pan in freezer to chill, at least 30 minutes. Press chocolate ice cream firmly over bottom and up side of chilled pan. Cover with foil or plastic wrap. Place in freezer; freeze until firm, about 3 hours. Set vanilla ice cream out to soften slightly. Spoon slightly softened vanilla ice cream into cavity of chocolate-lined pan. Press down to remove air pockets. Freeze until firm, about 3 hours. Set strawberry ice cream out to soften slightly. Spoon slightly softened strawberry ice cream on top of vanilla ice cream. Freeze until firm, about 3 hours. Place a medium serving plate or platter in freezer to chill, at least 30 minutes. In a small bowl, whip cream until soft peaks form; set aside. To unmold, dip frozen mold quickly in and out of lukewarm water to depth of contents. Invert mold onto chilled plate or platter; remove mold. Working quickly, frost with whipped cream; sprinkle with almonds. Serve immediately or return frosted mold to freezer. To serve, decorate with strawberries; cut into wedges. Makes 12 to 15 servings.

Make-Your-Own Watermelon

Stimulate conversation with this outstanding molded confection.

**1 qt. pistachio ice cream or
  lime sherbet, slightly softened**
1/4 cup semisweet chocolate pieces

**1 qt. raspberry sherbet or
  pink peppermint ice cream**

Place an 8-cup bombe or melon shaped mold in freezer to chill, at least 30 minutes. Line inside of chilled mold with a 1-inch layer of slightly softened pistachio ice cream or lime sherbet. Cover with foil or plastic wrap. Place in freezer; freeze until firm, about 3 hours. Cut chocolate pieces in half. Stir raspberry sherbet or pink peppermint ice cream to soften slightly; stir in cut chocolate pieces. Spoon into center of mold. Freeze until firm, about 3 hours. Place a medium platter or tray in freezer to chill, about 30 minutes. To unmold, dip mold quickly in and out of lukewarm water to depth of contents. Invert onto chilled platter or tray. To serve, cut into slices. Makes 8 to 10 servings.

Frozen Melba Mold

Elegant frozen version of the classic peach melba.

22 graham crackers, crushed (1-1/2 cups)
1/3 cup butter or margarine, melted
3 tablespoons sugar
1 (16-oz.) can sliced peaches
**1 (10-oz.) pkg. frozen raspberries,
  thawed**

1 qt. vanilla ice cream, slightly softened
1 teaspoon cornstarch
1/4 cup port wine
Whipped cream, if desired

In a medium bowl, combine graham cracker crumbs, butter or margarine and sugar. Press over bottom and 1 to 1-1/2 inches up side of a 9-inch springform pan; refrigerate. Thoroughly drain peaches, reserving juice for another use. Cut drained peaches into 3/4-inch pieces; set aside. Thoroughly drain raspberries reserving juice; set aside. Spoon softened ice cream into a large bowl. Carefully swirl cut peaches and drained raspberries through ice cream. Spoon into chilled crumb-lined pan. Cover with foil or plastic wrap. Place in freezer; freeze 6 hours or overnight. In a small saucepan, dissolve cornstarch in reserved raspberry juice. Cook and stir over medium heat until thickened and translucent. Stir in wine. Cool to room temperature. To serve, remove side from springform pan. Decorate frozen mold with whipped cream, if desired. Cut into 8 to 10 wedges. Spoon raspberry sauce over wedges. Makes 10 to 12 servings.

Banana-Brittle Ring

Start this early in the day to give each layer time to freeze solid.

1 qt. banana ice cream, slightly softened	**1 cup fudge sauce for topping, if desired**
1/2 cup fudge sauce	**1 cup whipping cream**
1 qt. chocolate-chip ice cream,	**1/2 cup crushed peanut brittle**
slightly softened	

Press banana ice cream about 1/2-inch thick on bottom and sides of a 6-1/2 cup ring mold. Cover with foil or plastic wrap. Place in freezer; freeze until firm, about 3 hours. Spoon 1/2 cup fudge sauce evenly over banana ice cream; freeze until firm, about 1 hour. Spoon chocolate-chip ice cream over frozen fudge sauce; press down lightly. Return to freezer; freeze until firm, about 3 hours. Place a medium serving plate or platter in freezer to chill, at least 30 minutes. If desired, pour 1 cup fudge sauce for topping into a pitcher; set aside. In a small bowl, whip cream until soft peaks form; set aside. To unmold, dip frozen mold quickly in and out of lukewarm water to depth of contents. Invert mold onto chilled plate or platter; remove mold. Working quickly, frost frozen mold with whipped cream; sprinkle with crushed peanut brittle. Serve immediately or return frosted mold to freezer until serving time. Let guests pour fudge sauce over individual servings, if desired. Makes 8 to 10 servings.

Macaroon-Fudge Loaf

For ease in slicing, place the loaf in the refrigerator about 15 minutes before serving.

12 (2-inch) chewy macaroons	**1 teaspoon vanilla extract**
1 (4-oz.) pkg. sweet baking chocolate	**1/2 cup chopped pecans**
2 eggs	**1 cup whipping cream**
4 cups sifted powdered sugar	

Line an 8" x 4" loaf pan with waxed paper, letting paper extend over edges. Grease waxed paper with soft butter or margarine. Use your fingers to crumble macaroons into small pieces. Press half of crumbled macaroons on bottom of waxed paper lined pan; reserve remaining macaroon crumbs. Refrigerate lined pan about 15 minutes. Place chocolate in top of double boiler. Melt over simmering water; set aside. In a large bowl, beat eggs. Stir in powdered sugar, melted chocolate and vanilla; beat until smooth. Stir in pecans. Spoon into chilled macaroon-lined pan. In a small bowl, whip cream until soft peaks form. Fold in reserved macaroon crumbs. Spoon over chocolate filling. Cover pan with foil or plastic wrap. Place in freezer; freeze until firm, 4 to 5 hours. To unmold, grasp waxed paper and lift molded loaf from pan; remove paper. Cut in crosswise slices. Makes 8 to 10 servings.

Frozen Chocolate-Buttercream Cups

This delicate, smooth confection is truly supreme!

2 (1-oz.) squares semisweet chocolate
1/2 cup butter
1 cup powdered sugar, sifted
3 egg yolks

1 teaspoon vanilla extract
3 egg whites
1/2 cup chocolate cookie crumbs
Whipped cream for decoration, if desired

Line 9 muffin cups with fluted paper baking cups; set aside. Melt chocolate over hot water or in microwave; set aside. In a small bowl, cream butter and powdered sugar until fluffy. Beat in egg yolks until thickened, about 5 minutes. Stir in melted chocolate and vanilla. In a medium bowl, beat egg whites until stiff but not dry. Fold into chocolate mixture. Spoon half of chocolate mixture evenly into paper-lined muffin pans. Sprinkle evenly with half of chocolate cookie crumbs. Spoon in remaining chocolate mixture; top with remaining crumbs. Cover with foil or plastic wrap. Place in freezer; freeze until firm, 2 to 4 hours. Decorate with dollops of whipped cream, if desired. Makes 9 servings.

Coconut Freeze

Fresh coconut will enhance the flavor.

1/3 cup sugar
3/4 cup water
1 cup freshly grated coconut or
   finely chopped flaked coconut
1 teaspoon vanilla extract

1/4 cup finely chopped candied fruits
1 cup whipping cream
16 vanilla wafers, finely crushed
   (1/2 cup)
9 or 10 maraschino cherries

In a small saucepan, combine sugar and water. Stir over medium heat until mixture comes to a boil. Continue to boil 5 minutes without stirring. Set aside until cool. Stir in coconut, vanilla and candied fruit, if desired. In a small bowl, whip cream until soft peaks form. Fold into coconut mixture. Line 9 or 10 muffin cups with fluted paper baking cups. Spoon half of coconut mixture evenly into paper-lined cups. Sprinkle with half of vanilla wafer crumbs. Spoon in remaining coconut mixture; top with remaining crumbs. Cover with foil or plastic wrap. Place in freezer; freeze until firm, 2 to 4 hours. To serve, place one molded mixture with cup on each plate. Top each with a cherry. Makes 9 or 10 servings.

Frozen Melba Cups

You'll want to serve this delightful flavor combination over and over again.

1 (10-oz.) pkg. frozen raspberries, thawed	**1 tablespoon lemon juice**
1 tablespoon light corn syrup	**1 (16-oz.) can sliced peaches, drained, chopped**
3/4 cup milk	**1/4 cup toasted chopped almonds**
1-1/2 cups miniature marshmallows	**1/2 cup whipping cream**

Line 12 muffin cups with fluted paper baking cups; set aside. In a small bowl, combine raspberries and corn syrup. Spoon raspberry mixture evenly into paper-lined cups. Cover with foil or plastic wrap. Place in freezer; freeze until firm, 2 to 4 hours. In a medium saucepan, combine milk and marshmallows. Stir over low heat until marshmallows melt. Stir in lemon juice, peaches and almonds. Cool to room temperature. In a small bowl, whip cream until soft peaks form. Fold into cooled peach mixture. Spoon over frozen raspberry mixture. Cover and freeze until firm, 1 to 3 hours. To serve, peel off paper. Place frozen mixture in sherbet glasses with raspberry mixture on top. Makes 12 servings.

_____ *How to Make Coconut Freeze* _____

1/Spoon half of coconut mixture into paper-lined muffin cups. Sprinkle with half of vanilla wafer crumbs. Repeat layers.

2/To serve, place 1 frozen serving with paper cup on each dessert plate. Decorate each with a cherry.

Fried Ice Cream

A real show stopper! Crisp on the outside and frozen on the inside.

6 scoops chocolate ice cream or
   vanilla ice cream
1 cup finely crushed graham crackers or
   vanilla wafers
1/4 teaspoon ground cinnamon

1 egg
1 tablespoon milk
Oil for deep-frying
Chocolate sauce, if desired

Place ice cream balls in a shallow 9-inch square pan. Cover with foil or plastic wrap. Place in freezer; freeze until very firm, at least 3 hours. In a small shallow bowl, combine crumbs and cinnamon. Quickly roll firm ice cream balls one at a time in crumbs; set crumbs aside. Freeze balls until very firm, 1 to 3 hours. In a small bowl, beat egg and milk until blended. Quickly roll coated ice cream balls in egg mixture; then in crumbs again. Return to freezer; freeze until firm, 1 to 3 hours. Pour oil 3 inches deep in a deep-fryer or medium saucepan. Heat oil to 375°F (190°C). At this temperature a 1-inch cube of bread will turn golden brown in 45 seconds. Use a slotted spoon to lower one ice cream ball at a time into hot oil. Fry until coating begins to brown, 8 to 10 seconds on each side. Serve immediately, plain or with chocolate sauce, if desired. Makes 6 servings.

Cherry-Almond Cream

Your small investment of time results in elegant dividends.

1 (21-oz.) can cherry pie filling
1 (14-oz.) can sweetened condensed milk
1/4 cup chopped blanched almonds, toasted
1 cup whipping cream

1/8 teaspoon almond extract
Toasted chopped almonds for decoration,
   if desired

Line 14 or 15 muffin cups with fluted paper baking cups or set aside 14 or 15 small individual molds. In a medium bowl, combine pie filling and sweetened condensed milk. Stir in 1/4 cup almonds. In a small bowl, whip cream until soft peaks form. Stir in almond extract. Fold into cherry mixture. Spoon into paper-lined muffin cups or individual molds. Cover with foil or plastic wrap. Place in freezer; freeze until firm, 2 to 4 hours. To serve, peel off paper; arrange on a platter. Decorate with additional almonds, if desired. Makes 14 or 15 servings.

*Crush graham crackers or cookies in a
plastic bag to save on clean-up time.*

Frozen Zabaglione

This heavenly concoction is even better when served with fresh sliced peaches or strawberries.

4 egg yolks, slightly beaten
1/3 cup sugar

1/2 cup Marsala wine
1 cup whipping cream

In bottom of double boiler, bring water almost to a boil over medium heat. Reduce heat to very low, keeping water just below boiling. In top of double boiler, combine slightly beaten egg yolks, sugar and wine. Place over hot water and beat with electric mixer until thick, 6 to 8 minutes. Set aside to cool 15 minutes. Line 9 or 10 muffin cups or custard cups with fluted paper baking cups; set aside. In a small bowl, whip cream until soft peaks form. Fold 3/4 of whipped cream into partially cooled egg mixture. Spoon egg mixture evenly into paper cups. Top each with a dollop of remaining whipped cream. Place in freezer; freeze until firm, 2 to 4 hours. To serve, peel off paper; serve immediately. Makes 9 or 10 servings.

Wallbanger Tortoni

Individually frozen desserts top off a special dinner.

2 tablespoons chopped blanched almonds
2 tablespoons flaked coconut
1 cup whipping cream
2 tablespoons diced candied orange peel

1 tablespoon Galliano liqueur
2 egg whites
1/2 cup sugar

Line 8 to 10 muffin cups with fluted paper baking cups; set aside. In a small skillet, stir almonds and coconut over low heat until toasted; set aside to cool. In a medium bowl, whip cream until stiff. Fold in candied orange peel, Galliano and toasted almonds and coconut. In a small bowl, beat egg whites until soft peaks form. Gradually beat in sugar until stiff but not dry. Fold beaten egg white mixture into whipped cream mixture. Spoon into paper-lined muffin cups. Cover with foil or plastic wrap. Place in freezer; freeze until firm, 2 to 4 hours. To serve, peel off paper; serve immediately. Makes 8 to 10 servings.

How to Fold in Beaten Egg Whites

When folding in beaten egg whites, use a rubber spatula to avoid breaking up air bubbles. Move the spatula down through the mixture, across the bottom of the bowl or pan, up through the mixture and across the top, skimming the surface. Repeat until no traces of egg white remain.

Soda Fountain & Bar Concoctions

There's no trick to making sundaes. Make them from ice cream and any of the toppings in this section. Crown them with whipped cream, chopped nuts and a cherry. If you are making more than one or two sundaes or sodas, scoop the ice cream ahead of time. Place the ice cream scoops in a shallow baking pan or on individual serving dishes. Cover with foil or plastic wrap and immediately return them to the freezer. Use a regular ice cream dipper to make round balls of ice cream or a special spade-type which makes thin oval shapes. A tablespoon can also be used to make oval scoops. To keep the ice cream from sticking, rinse your dipping tool in a glass of lukewarm water after making each scoop.

Parfaits are made ahead of time in tall slender parfait glasses. If you don't have these glasses, improvise with wine glasses or small goblets. Make alternate layers of ice cream and topping. Vanilla ice cream is excellent in parfaits, but be adventurous and try any of the dozens of flavors in this book. Or try commercial ice cream with some of our sauces or toppings.

Start an evening of entertaining off right by offering Bellini Freeze or Frozen Kir Spritzer. Bellini Freeze is a copy of a drink served to us in Venice. We modernized it by freezing the peach mixture and scoring it when partially frozen. Break the frozen cubes apart and place them in the refrigerator 10 to 15 minutes to soften slightly. To serve, pour Asti Spumante sparkling wine over the frozen cubes. Serve with a spoon. Frozen Kit Spritzer is an Americanized version of a popular French apertif. Freeze the wine-and-cassis mixture, then combine it with club soda or lemon-lime soda just before serving.

Classic Banana Split   *Photo on pages 2 and 3.*

Change this basic combination with different flavors of ice cream and toppings.

1 banana, split in half lengthwise
1 scoop vanilla ice cream
1 scoop chocolate ice cream
1 scoop strawberry ice cream
1 tablespoon chocolate syrup
1 tablespoon marshmallow creme

1 tablespoon strawberry preserves or
   Raspberry Topping, page 155
Whipped cream
Chopped nuts
3 maraschino cherries

Arrange half of banana on each side of a shallow oval dish. Place scoops of vanilla, chocolate and strawberry ice cream in a row between banana slices. Spoon chocolate syrup over vanilla ice cream, marshmallow over chocolate ice cream and strawberry preserves or Raspberry Topping over strawberry ice cream. Top each ice cream scoop with whipped cream, chopped nuts and a maraschino cherry. Serve immediately. Makes 1 serving.

Praline Parfait

This has the wonderful taste of pralines.

1 cup packed brown sugar
1/2 cup light corn syrup
1/2 cup half-and-half
1/4 cup butter or margarine
1/2 teaspoon vanilla extract

1/2 cup chopped pecans
1 qt. vanilla ice cream or
   coffee ice cream
Whipped cream for decoration

In a medium saucepan, combine brown sugar, corn syrup, half-and-half and butter or margarine. Stir over low heat until sugar dissolves. Let simmer 5 minutes. Stir in vanilla and pecans. Cool to room temperature. Place 6 to 8 parfait glasses or wine glasses in freezer to chill, at least 30 minutes. Arrange alternate layers of ice cream and sauce in chilled glasses. Cover with foil or plastic wrap. Place in freezer; freeze until firm, 2 to 4 hours. To serve, decorate each serving with whipped cream. Makes 6 to 8 servings.

Blueberry Melba

Create an eye-catching dessert with this combination.

1/2 cup sugar
1 tablespoon cornstarch
3/4 cup port wine
2 tablespoons lemon juice

1-1/2 cups fresh blueberries
6 fresh or canned peach halves
6 scoops vanilla ice cream

In a small saucepan, combine sugar and cornstarch. Stir in wine and lemon juice. Cook and stir over low heat until thickened and translucent. Stir in blueberries; simmer about 5 minutes. Cool to room temperature. To serve, arrange peach halves cut side up in 6 sherbet glasses. Top each with 1 scoop ice cream. Spoon cooled blueberry sauce evenly over each. Makes 6 servings.

Strawberry Sodas   *Photo on page 15.*

This must be served while the bubbles are still active.

1/2 cup cold milk	**Cold club soda**
1/4 cup strawberry syrup	**Whipped cream**
4 scoops strawberry ice cream	**2 maraschino cherries**

In a small bowl, stir milk into strawberry syrup. Pour evenly into two tall glasses. Add 1 scoop of ice cream to each glass. Pour a small amount of club soda into each glass. Press ice cream into club soda with back of a long-handled spoon. Add second scoop of ice cream to each glass. Fill glasses with soda. Garnish each with whipped cream and a cherry. Serve immediately. Makes 2 servings.

Variations

Raspberry Sodas: Substitute Raspberry Topping, page 155, for strawberry syrup. Use strawberry ice cream or vanilla ice cream.
Coffee Sodas: Substitute 2 tablespoons Coffee Syrup, page 156, for syrup. Use chocolate ice cream or coffee ice cream.
Chocolate Sodas: Substitute chocolate syrup and chocolate ice cream for strawberry syrup and strawberry ice cream.

Fudge Sundaes

Mix or match your favorite ice creams with homemade or commercial toppings.

1 qt. vanilla ice cream or	**Whipped cream**
chocolate ice cream	**Chopped nuts**
3/4 to 1 cup fudge sauce, warm or	**6 maraschino cherries**
room temperature	

Make 6 large or 12 small scoops of ice cream. Divide evenly among six sherbet glasses. Spoon sauce evenly over ice cream. Top each with whipped cream, nuts and a cherry; serve immediately. Makes 6 servings.

Variations

Caramel Sundae: Use butter-pecan or vanilla ice cream with Burnt-Sugar Sauce, page 155.
Butterscotch Crunch Sundae: Use vanilla ice cream with Peanut Crunch Topping, page 155.
Pineapple Coconut Sundae: Use Mauna Loa Topping, page 156, with Banana-Rum Ice Cream, page 81, or Banana Macadamia Nut Ice Cream, page 81.

1/Pour half of strawberry mixture into a tall glass. Add 1 scoop of ice cream and a little club soda. Stir with a long spoon.

2/Add second scoop of ice cream to glass. Fill glass with soda. Garnish with whipped cream and a cherry.

How to Make Strawberry Sodas

Grasshopper Ice Cream

Flavors are borrowed from the famous grasshopper pie.

1 cup dairy sour cream
1/4 cup green crème de menthe
3 tablespoons white crème de cacao

1 (7-oz.) jar marshmallow creme
1 cup whipping cream
1 to 2 cups chocolate sauce

In a small bowl, stir sour cream until smooth. Gradually stir in crème de menthe and crème de cacao; set aside. Spoon marshmallow into a medium bowl. Gradually stir in sour cream mixture. Stir in whipping cream. Pour into a 9" x 5" loaf pan or several undivided ice trays. Cover with foil or plastic wrap. Place in freezer; freeze until firm. Stir 2 or 3 times with a fork or spoon while freezing. Serve with chocolate sauce. Makes about 6 servings.

Green Silk

This drink is so thick you can serve it with a spoon.

1 ripe avocado, quartered
3/4 cup chilled pineapple juice

4 large scoops orange sherbet

In blender or food processor, combine all ingredients. Process until smooth. Pour into 2 or 3 wine glasses or champagne glasses. Serve immediately. Makes 2 or 3 servings.

Quickie Fruit Drink

Makes a sweltry day tolerable.

1 large banana, cut in pieces
1 cup milk

2 large scoops orange or pineapple sherbet
Ground nutmeg

Combine banana, milk and sherbet in blender or food processor. Blend until smooth. Pour into 2 large glasses. Sprinkle with nutmeg. Makes 2 servings.

Creamy Piña Colada

You'll find cans of cream of coconut in beverage or gourmet sections of supermarkets.

1/4 cup canned pineapple juice
3 tablespoons cream of coconut

3 tablespoons rum
3 large scoops vanilla ice cream

In blender or food processor, combine all ingredients. Blend until smooth and creamy. Pour evenly into 2 sherbets glasses or cocktail glasses. Serve immediately. Makes 2 servings.

Orange Smoothie

Serve it with a spoon, or drink it like a milk shake.

1 qt. vanilla ice cream
1 (6-oz.) can orange juice concentrate,
 partially thawed

2 tablespoons orange flavored liqueur,
 if desired

Puree half of ingredients in blender or food processor until well blended but not thawed. Pour evenly into four to six 8-ounce glasses. Repeat with remaining ingredients. Serve immediately. Makes 4 to 6 servings.

Frozen Peach Daiquiri

Peach-flavored version of a favorite drink.

2 fresh peaches, peeled, chopped
1 (6-oz.) can frozen daiquiri mix,
   partially thawed

4 large scoops peach ice cream or
   vanilla ice cream
1/2 cup light rum

In blender or food processor, combine peaches and daiquiri mix. Blend until almost smooth. Add ice cream and rum; blend until almost smooth. Pour evenly into four 7- or 8-ounce glasses. Serve immediately. Makes 4 drinks.

Frozen Banana Daiquiri

Banana lovers will like this drink.

2 large bananas
1 (6-oz.) can frozen daiquiri mix,
   partially thawed

4 large scoops banana ice cream or
   vanilla ice cream
1/2 cup light rum

In blender or food processor, process bananas and daiquiri mix until almost smooth. Add ice cream and rum; blend until almost smooth. Pour into four 7- or 8-ounce glasses. Serve immediately. Makes 4 drinks.

Frozen Strawberry Daiquiri

Another version of the popular strawberry drink.

1/2 cup sliced fresh strawberries
1 (6-oz.) can frozen daiquiri mix,
   partially thawed

4 large scoops strawberry ice cream or
   vanilla ice cream
1/2 cup light rum

In blender or food processor, combine strawberries and daiquiri mix. Blend until almost smooth. Add ice cream and rum; blend until almost smooth. Pour into four 7- or 8-ounce glasses. Serve immediately. Makes 4 drinks.

For an easy decoration, sprinkle grated semisweet chocolate or chocolate curls on top of coffee or chocolate flavored sundaes or parfaits.

Ice Cream After-Dinner Drinks

Choose your favorite flavor for a combination dessert and after-dinner drink.

Grasshopper:
2 tablespoons green crème de menthe
2 tablespoons white crème de cocoa

2 large scoops vanilla ice cream
Whipped cream

Mocha:
2 tablespoons coffee-flavored liqueur
2 tablespoons white crème de cocoa

2 large scoops vanilla ice cream
Whipped cream

Brandied Peach:
2 tablespoons brandy
2 tablespoons orange-flavored liqueur

2 large scoops peach ice cream
Whipped cream

Amaretto:
2 tablespoons Amaretto liqueur
1 large scoop orange sherbet

1 large scoop vanilla ice cream
Whipped cream

In blender, combine liqueurs and ice cream; blend until smooth. Pour into 2 sherbet glasses or wine glasses. Top with whipped cream. Makes 2 servings.

Bloody Mary Frappé

Begin your Sunday brunch with this perfect combination.

3 cups tomato juice
1 tablespoon sugar
1/8 teaspoon pepper
1 tablespoon lime juice
1/4 teaspoon salt
1 teaspoon grated onion

1/2 teaspoon celery salt
1 tablespoon Worcestershire sauce
1/8 teaspoon garlic powder
Dash hot pepper sauce
1/4 cup vodka

Combine ingredients in a large bowl. Pour into ice cream canister. Freeze in ice cream maker according to manufacturer's directions. Mixture should be slushy but slightly firm. Spoon into 5 wine glasses. Serve with a spoon and a straw, or suggest guests drink mixture as it melts. **Freezer method:** Pour prepared mixture into a 9" x 5" loaf pan or several undivided ice trays. Cover with foil or plastic wrap. Place in freezer; freeze until firm, 3 to 6 hours. Scrape frozen mixture with a fork until pieces resemble finely crushed ice. For a smoother texture, freeze prepared mixture until firm; break into small pieces. Spoon into chilled food processor bowl. Beat with metal blade until smooth and fluffy but not thawed. Serve immediately. Makes 5 servings.

Grasshopper After-Dinner Drink

Bellini Freeze

Frozen version of a famous Venetian drink.

4 fresh ripe peaches, peeled
1/2 cup sugar
2 tablespoons almond liqueur

1 (750-milliliter) bottle Asti Spumante
or other sweet sparkling white wine,
chilled

Remove and discard peach pits. In blender or food processor, puree peaches and sugar until almost smooth. Add almond liqueur; process 2 to 3 seconds to blend. Pour into a 9" x 5" loaf pan. Cover with foil or plastic wrap. Place in freezer; freeze until almost firm, 1 to 3 hours. Cut 3 lengthwise rows and 8 crosswise rows through partially frozen mixture. Replace cover and return to freezer; freeze until firm, 1 to 3 hours. Place in refrigerator to soften slightly 10 to 15 minutes before serving. To serve, place 3 pieces of frozen mixture in each of 8 sherbet glasses or champagne glasses. Pour Asti Spumante or other sweet white wine over frozen mixture. Serve with a spoon. Makes 8 servings.

Wine Slush

An absolutely divine dessert that's almost soft enough to drink.

1 cup sugar
1 cup water
1 teaspoon grated orange peel

1 cup Burgundy wine
1 cup orange juice
1/4 cup lemon juice

In a small saucepan, combine sugar, water and orange peel. Stir over medium heat until mixture comes to a boil. Without stirring, simmer over low heat 5 minutes. Place a fine strainer over a medium bowl. Pour syrup through strainer to remove orange peel. Cool to room temperature. Stir in wine, orange juice and lemon juice. Pour into ice cream canister. Freeze in ice cream maker according to manufacturer's directions. **Freezer method:** Pour prepared mixture into a 9" x 5" loaf pan or several individual ice trays. Cover with foil or plastic wrap. Place in freezer; freeze until almost firm, 1 to 3 hours. Stir with a fork or spoon 2 or 3 times while freezing. Serve while slushy. Makes 3 to 4 cups.

1/When mixture is partially frozen, make 24 pieces by cutting 3 lengthwise rows and 8 crosswise rows.

2/Place 3 pieces of frozen peach mixture into each glass. Fill with Asti Spumante; serve immediately.

How to Make Bellini Freeze

Frozen Kir Spritzer

Tastes like a wine cooler.

2 cups dry white wine
1/4 cup sugar
2 tablespoons lemon juice

1/2 cup crème de cassis
3 (12-oz.) cans club soda or
    lemon-lime soda

In a small saucepan, combine wine, sugar and lemon juice. Stir over low heat until sugar dissolves. Cool to room temperature. Stir in cassis. Pour into a 9" x 5" loaf pan or several undivided ice trays. Cover with foil or plastic wrap. Place in freezer; freeze until almost firm. 1 to 3 hours. Break into small pieces. Spoon into a chilled large bowl or chilled food processor bowl. Beat with electric mixer or metal food processor blade until fine-grained but not thawed. Return beaten mixture to pan and freeze until almost firm, 1 to 3 hours. To serve, scoop frozen mixture into 5 or 6 tall glasses. Fill glasses with club soda or lemon-lime soda. Makes 5 or 6 servings.

Favorite Fudge Sauce   Photo on page 15.

Quick topping for sundaes and parfaits.

1/2 cup sugar
1/4 cup unsweetened cocoa powder
1/2 cup light corn syrup

1/4 cup half-and-half
2 tablespoons butter or margarine
1/2 teaspoon vanilla extract

In a small saucepan, combine sugar and cocoa. Stir in corn syrup and half-and-half. Stir over medium heat until mixture comes to a boil. Stirring occasionally, simmer 3 minutes. Stir in butter or margarine and vanilla. Serve warm or cold. Makes about 1 cup.

Praline Sauce

Rich and gooey like pecan pie.

1 cup packed brown sugar
1/4 cup light corn syrup
1/2 cup half-and-half

2 tablespoons butter or margarine
1/2 cup coarsely chopped pecans
1/2 teaspoon vanilla extract

In a small saucepan, combine brown sugar, corn syrup and half-and-half. Cook and stir over medium heat until thickened, 7 to 8 minutes. Stir in butter or margarine, pecans and vanilla. Cool slightly. Serve warm. Makes about 1-1/3 cups.

Maple-Walnut Sauce

Serve as a topping or flavoring for sundaes, sodas or parfaits.

1 cup maple-flavored syrup
1/4 cup lightly packed brown sugar
1 tablespoon butter or margarine
1/4 cup water

1/4 cup half-and-half
1/4 teaspoon vanilla extract
1/4 cup chopped walnuts

In a heavy medium saucepan, combine maple syrup, brown sugar, butter or margarine and water. Stir over medium heat until mixture comes to a boil. Over low heat, simmer until slightly thickened, about 10 minutes. Stir in half-and-half, vanilla and walnuts. Cool to room temperature. Makes about 1 cup.

Hot sauces are ready to use in seconds when poured into a glass measuring cup and heated in your microwave oven. Make hot fudge or hot butterscotch sauces ahead and heat them this way.

Raspberry Topping

For raspberry ripple ice cream, swirl 1/4 cup of this topping into one quart vanilla ice cream.

1 (10-oz.) pkg. frozen raspberries, thawed
1 teaspoon cornstarch

2 tablespoons cold water
1/4 cup currant jelly

Puree raspberries in blender or food processor; set aside. In a small saucepan, dissolve cornstarch in cold water. Stir in raspberry puree. Stir over medium heat until mixture comes to a boil. Stirring constantly, simmer over low heat 1 minute. Stir in currant jelly until melted. Pour through a fine strainer to remove seeds, if desired. Cool to room temperature. Makes about 1 cup.

Brandied Apricot-Nut Topping

Use as a sundae topping or between layers of ice cream in a parfait.

1 cup apricot jam
2 tablespoons orange juice

1/4 cup chopped almonds, toasted
1 tablespoon apricot brandy

In a small saucepan, combine apricot jam and orange juice. Stir over low heat until jam dissolves. Stir in almonds and brandy. Serve warm. Makes about 1-1/4 cups.

Peanut Crunch Topping

Peanutty variation of hot caramel sauce.

1/2 cup butter
2 cups packed brown sugar
1/3 cup half-and-half

3/4 cup peanut butter
1/4 cup chopped peanuts
1/2 teaspoon vanilla extract

Melt butter in a medium saucepan. Stir in brown sugar, half-and-half and peanut butter. Stir over low heat until smooth. Stir in peanuts and vanilla. Serve warm. Makes about 2-3/4 cups.

Burnt-Sugar Sauce

Serve on butter-pecan ice cream or angel food cake.

1 cup sugar
1/3 cup boiling water
1 tablespoon butter or margarine

1 teaspoon vanilla extract
1/3 cup half-and-half

In a heavy 10-inch skillet, heat sugar over medium heat until melted around edge. Immediately reduce heat to very low. Cook, stirring constantly, until sugar is completely dissolved and turns a light amber color. Gradually stir in boiling water. Stir in butter or margarine. Cook and stir until smooth and slightly thickened, 2 to 3 minutes. Set aside to cool 5 minutes. Stir in vanilla and half-and-half. Refrigerate until serving time. Makes about 1 cup.

Chocolate-Marshmallow Sauce

Stir just before serving to redistribute the marshmallow mixture.

2 (1-oz.) squares semisweet chocolate
1/2 cup milk
1/4 cup sugar

1 tablespoon butter or margarine
1 cup miniature marshmallows
1/2 teaspoon vanilla extract

In a heavy small saucepan, combine chocolate, milk, sugar and butter or margarine. Stir over low heat until chocolate melts. Stir in marshmallows and vanilla until marshmallows melt. Stir again before serving. Serve warm or cool. Makes about 1 cup.

Coffee Syrup

Spoon about one tablespoon coffee syrup into each milkshake or soda.

3/4 cup sugar
1/4 cup light corn syrup

2 tablespoons instant coffee powder
1/2 cup water

In a medium saucepan, combine sugar and corn syrup. Dissolve coffee powder in water; add to sugar mixture. Stir over medium heat until mixture comes to a boil. Stirring occasionally, simmer over low heat 6 minutes. Cool to room temperature. Makes about 1 cup.

Mauna Loa Topping

Serve on Banana-Macadamia-Nut Ice Cream or Banana-Rum Ice Cream, page 81.

1/4 cup sugar
1 teaspoon cornstarch
1 (8-oz.) can crushed pineapple with juice
2 tablespoons water

1 teaspoon lemon juice
1 tablespoon butter or margarine
2 tablespoons flaked coconut
1/8 teaspoon almond extract

In a small saucepan, combine sugar and cornstarch. Stir in crushed pineapple with juice, water and lemon juice; add butter or margarine. Stir over medium heat until mixture comes to a boil. Simmer over low heat 2 minutes. Stir in flaked coconut and almond extract. Serve warm or cold. Makes about 1-1/4 cups.

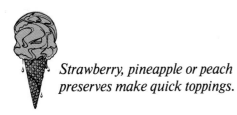

Strawberry, pineapple or peach preserves make quick toppings.

Index

A

Acapulco Mocha Pie 102
After-Dinner Drinks, Ice Cream 150, 151
Alaska, Aloha Baked 106, 107
Alaska, Baked 106
Alcoholic beverages, see
    Preparing the Brine
    Soda Fountain & Bar Concoctions
Almond Cream, Cherry 142
Almond Mousse, Burnt 132, 133
Aloha Baked Alaska 106, 107
Anytime Tropical Freeze 86
Appetizer
    Gazpacho Frappé 98, 99
    Green Chowder Frappé 100
Apple Ice Cream, Candy 76, 77
Apple Yogurt, Frozen 78
Apple-Cheese Ice Cream 75
Apple-Walnut Custard 76
Applesauce Freeze, Spicy 78
Apricot Cream Mold 133
Apricot Freeze, Double 69
Apricot-Lemon Cream 69
Apricot-Nut Topping, Brandied 155
Apricot-Pineapple Yogurt, Frozen 70
Avo-Orange Ice Cream 92
Avocado Frozen Yogurt 92
Avocado-Orange Cups 52, 53

B

Baked Alaska 106
Baked Alaska, Aloha 106, 107
Bali Hai Cream 80
Banana Daiquiri, Frozen 149
Banana Ice Cream, Peanut Butter 80
Banana Macadamia Nut Ice Cream 81
Banana Split, Classic 3-4, 145
Banana-Brittle Ring 139
Banana-Orange Sorbet 83
Banana-Orange Yogurt 81
Banana-Rum Ice Cream 81
Bananas, Frozen 115
Bar Concoctions, Soda Fountain & 144-156
Basic Vanilla Ice Cream 19
Bayou Crunch, Frozen 130
Beachcomber's Delight 83
Beaten Egg Whites, How to Fold in 143
Bellini Freeze 152, 153
Berries, see Fruits of the Vine
Berry Sorbet, Cherry 66
Bloody Mary Frappé 151
Blueberry Melba 145
Blueberry Sorbet 48
Blueberry-Orange Yogurt 48
Bombe, Defined 16
Bombe, Peach 135
Bonbons, Ice Cream 116
Boysenberry Ice Cream 49
Brandied Apricot-Nut Topping 155
Brandied Cherry Ice Cream 65
Brine, Preparing the 11
Brittle Ring, Banana 139
Brownie Igloos 104
Burnt Almond Mousse 132, 133
Burnt Sugar Sauce 155
Butter-Pecan Ice Cream 122
Buttercream Cups, Frozen Chocolate 140
Butterscotch Ice Cream 123
Butterscotch Peanut Butter Ice Cream 122
Butterscotch Pudding Ice Cream 123
Butterscotch-Pecan Ripple 122

C

Café au Lait Ice Cream 32, 33
Cake Mold, Neapolitan 136
Cake, Ice Cream 116, 117
Cakes, see Pies & Cakes 101-111
Calorie Counter's Ice Cream 22
Candied Orange Pineapple Cream 126
Candies, Nuts & Caramels 121-130
Candy-Apple Ice Cream 76, 77
Cantaloupe Ice 96
Cantaloupe Sherbet 94, 95
Cantaloupe-Wine Sorbet 95
Cappucino Ice Cream 31
Caramel Ice Cream 130
Caramels, Nuts, Candies & 121-130
Care of Ice Cream Maker 8
Cereal Ring, Rocky Road 120
Cheese Ice Cream, Apple 75
Cheesecake Ice Cream, Cherry 65
Cheesecake Ice Cream, Lemon 55
Cheesecake, Frozen Lime 111
Cheesecake, Frozen Mocha 111
Cherries Jubilee 66, 67
Cherry Cheesecake Ice Cream 65
Cherry Ice Cream, Brandied 65
Cherry-Almond Cream 142
Cherry-Berry Sorbet 66
Cherry-Chocolate Swirl 68
Children, see Just For Kids 112-120
Chip Ice Cream, Tangerine 60
Chocolate Chip Mint Ice Cream 26, 108
Chocolate Cloud 105
Chocolate Ice Cream Sandwiches 113
Chocolate Ice Cream, Old-Fashioned 25, 117
Chocolate Ice Cream, Ranch House 25
Chocolate Ice Cream, Soft 28
Chocolate Marshmallow Sauce 156
Chocolate Pudding Ice Cream 29
Chocolate Sherbet, Easy 30
Chocolate Sherbet, Mandarin 30
Chocolate Swirl, Cherry 68
Chocolate, Coffee & Tea 24-34
Chocolate-Buttercream Cups, Frozen 140
Chocolate-Mint Meringue Pie 105
Chocolate-Mint Truffle Mold 136, 137
Chowder Frappé, Green 100
Cider Sorbet, Mulled 77
Citrus Fruits 50-61
Citrus Tea Ice 34
Classic Banana Split 3-4, 145
Cloud, Chocolate 105
Clown, Ice Cream 113
Coats a Spoon, How to Tell When a Mixture 23
Coco-Damia Ice Cream 82, 87
Coconut Freeze 140. 141
Coconut Freeze, Cream of 88
Coconut Sherbet 87
Coconut Yogurt, Mango 82, 86
Coconut, also see
    Bali Hai Cream 80
    Beachcomber's Delight 83
    Coco-Damia Ice Cream 82
    Frozen Bayou Crunch 130
Coffee & Tea, Chocolate, 24-34
Coffee Ice Cream, Irish 31
Coffee Ice Cream, Toffee 31
Coffee Syrup 156
Cooler, Watermelon-Wine 98
Cranberry Sherbet, Orange 43
Cranberry-Orange Ice 42
Cranberry-Wine Sorbet 42, 43
Cream Mold, Apricot 133
Cream Sherbet, Orange 52
Cream of Coconut Freeze 88

Cream, Apricot-Lemon 69
Cream, Bali Hai 80
Cream, Candied Orange Pineapple 126
Cream, Cherry-Almond 142
Cream, Frozen Lemon 54
Cream, Frozen Nectarine 72
Cream, Grand Marnier 54
Cream, Magic Lemon 55
Cream, Mardi Gras 125
Cream, Peanut Butter Fudge 25
Cream, Pronto Strawberry 36
Cream, Strawberry 36
Cream, Strawberry Italian 38
Cream, also see Ice Cream
Creamy Lime Sherbet 58
Creamy Piña Colada 148
Creamy Strawberry Yogurt 38
Crème, Mexican Mocha 33
Creme, Raspberry Yogurt 44
Crenshaw Ice Cream 96
Crown Vanilla, Royal 19
Crunch Mold, Peanut 132
Crunch Topping, Peanut 155
Crunch, Frozen Bayou 130
Cups, Avocado-Orange 52, 53
Cups, Frozen Chocolate-Buttercream 140
Cups, Frozen Melba 141
Cups, Praline 128, 129
Custard Ice Cream, Peach 64
Custard, Apple-Walnut 76
Custard, Frozen 23
Custard, Frozen Rhubarb 100

D

Daiquiri, Frozen Banana 149
Daiquiri, Frozen Peach 149
Daiquiri, Frozen Strawberry 149
Date Yogurt, Sun 90
Date-Nut Ice Cream 90
Definitions of Frozen Desserts 16
Delight, Beachcomber's 83
Desserts, Molded Frozen 131-143
Dinner Drinks, Ice Cream After 150, 151
Double Apricot Freeze 69
Dreamy Lime Ice Cream 58
Drink, Quickie Fruit 148
Drinks, Ice Cream After Dinner 150, 151

E

Easy Chocolate Sherbet 30
Easy Fruit Pops 118
Egg Whites, How to Fold in Beaten 143
Eggless Ice Cream
    Apricot-Lemon Cream 69
    Avo-Orange Ice Cream 92
    Butterscotch Peanut Butter 122
    Candied Orange Pineapple Cream 126
    Candy-Apple Ice Cream 76, 77
    Cappucino Ice Cream 31
    Cherry Cheesecake Ice Cream 65
    Cherry-Almond Cream 142
    Date-Nut Ice Cream 90
    Frozen Lemon Cream 54
    Ginger-Pear Ice Cream 70, 71
    Heritage Peach Ice Cream 63
    Magic Lemon Cream 55
    Mocha Ice Cream 32
    Peanut Butter Fudge Cream 25
    Pronto Strawberry Cream 36
    Pumpkin Ice Cream 100
    Quick Vanilla Ice Cream 20
    Ranch House Chocolate Ice Cream 25
    Soft Chocolate Ice Cream 28
    Soft Vanilla Ice Cream 20
Eggnog-Pumpkin Pie, Frozen 103, 108

Index

F

Favorite Fudge Sauce 154
Fold in Beaten Egg Whites, How to 143
Framboise Sherbet 45
Frappé Defined 16
Frappé, Bloody Mary 151
Frappé, Gazpacho 98, 99
Frappé, Green Chowder 100
Freeze Ice Cream, How to 10
Freeze, Anytime Tropical 86
Freeze, Bellini 152, 153
Freeze, Coconut 140. 141
Freeze, Cream of Coconut 88
Freeze, Double Apricot 69
Freeze, Lemon-Lime 57
Freeze, Spicy Applesauce 78
Fresh Peach Ice Cream 63
Fresh Plum Ice Cream 73
Fresh Plum Sorbet 74
Fresh Raspberry Ice Cream 45
Fried Ice Cream 142
Frozen Apple Yogurt 78
Frozen Apricot-Pineapple Yogurt 70
Frozen Banana Daiquiri 149
Frozen Bananas 115
Frozen Bayou Crunch 130
Frozen Chocolate-Buttercream Cups 140
Frozen Custard 23
Frozen Desserts, Definitions of 16
Frozen Eggnog-Pumpkin Pie 103, 108
Frozen Kir Spritzer 153
Frozen Lemon Cream 54
Frozen Lime Cheesecake 111
Frozen Melba Cups 141
Frozen Melba Mold 138
Frozen Mocha Cheesecake 111
Frozen Nectarine Cream 72
Frozen Peach Daiquiri 149
Frozen Rhubarb Custard 100
Frozen Strawberry Daiquiri 149
Frozen Strawberry Sour Cream 39
Frozen Strawberry Wine 41
Frozen Strawberry Yogurt 38
Frozen Yogurt, Avocado 92
Frozen Yogurt, Italian-Style 22
Frozen Zabaglione 143
Fruit Drink, Quickie 148
Fruit Pops, Easy 118
Fruit Salad Pops 118, 119
Fruits of the Vine 35-49
Fruits, Citrus 50-61
Fruits, Orchard 62-78
Fruits, Tropical 79-92
Frutti Sorbet, Tutti 68
Fudge Cream, Peanut Butter 25
Fudge Ice Cream 30
Fudge Loaf, Macaroon 139
Fudge Ripple Ice Cream 28, 29
Fudge Sauce, Favorite 154
Fudge Sundaes 146

G

Gazpacho Frappé 98, 99
Gelatin
  Apricot-Lemon Cream 69
  Avocado-Orange Cups 52, 53
  Coconut Sherbet 87
  Creamy Lime Sherbet 58
  Creamy Strawberry Yogurt 38
  Date-Nut Ice Cream 90
  Frozen Custard 23
  Orange-Cranberry Sherbet 43
  Orange-Pineapple Yogurt 51
  Peachy Orange Yogurt 65
  Soft Chocolate Ice Cream 28
  Soft Vanilla Ice Cream 20
  Spicy Applesauce Freeze 78

Strawberry Ice 40
Strawberry Sherbet 39
Tangerine Sherbet 61
Ginger Tea Ice Cream 34
Ginger-Pear Ice Cream 70, 71
Gingerbread Roll 108, 110
Golden Glow Yogurt 99
Golden State Sherbet 52
Graham Cracker Sandwiches,
  Peanut Butter 114, 115
Grand Marnier Cream 54
Grape Punch Sorbet 47
Grape Sherbet 46, 47
Grape Slush 46
Grape-Yogurt Pops 119
Grapefruit Sorbet, Minty 56, 57
Grapes, see Fruits of the Vine 35-49
Grasshopper Ice Cream 147
Green Chowder Frappé 100
Green Silk 148

H

Harvey Wallbanger Pie 104
Hawaiian Sorbet 91
Hazelnut Ice Cream Italiano 124, 125
Heritage Peach Ice Cream 63
Honey Yogurt, Orange 51, 108
How to Fold in Beaten Egg Whites 143
How to Freeze Ice Cream 10
How to Tell When a Mixture Coats
  a Spoon 23

I

Ice Cream After-Dinner Drinks 150, 151
Ice Cream Bonbons 116
Ice Cream Cake 116, 117
Ice Cream Clown 113
Ice Cream Defined 16
Ice Cream Italiano, Hazelnut 124, 125
Ice Cream Maker, Care of 8
Ice Cream Maker, Selecting an 7
Ice Cream Roll 110
Ice Cream Sandwiches, Chocolate 113
Ice Cream, also see Cream
Ice Cream
  Apple-Cheese 75
  Avo-Orange 92
  Banana Macadamia Nut 81
  Banana-Rum 81
  Basic Vanilla 19
  Boysenberry 49
  Brandied Cherry 65
  Butter-Pecan 122
  Butterscotch 123
  Butterscotch Peanut Butter 122
  Butterscotch Pudding 123
  Café au Lait 32, 33
  Calorie Counter's 22
  Candy-Apple 76, 77
  Cappucino 31
  Caramel 130
  Cherry Cheesecake 65
  Chocolate Chip Mint 26, 108
  Chocolate Pudding 29
  Coco-Damia 82, 87
  Crenshaw 96
  Date-Nut 90
  Dreamy Lime 58
  Fresh Peach 63
  Fresh Plum 73
  Fresh Raspberry 45
  Fried 142
  Fudge 30
  Fudge Ripple 28, 29
  Ginger Tea 34
  Ginger-Pear 70, 71
  Grasshopper 147

Heritage Peach 63
Irish Coffee 31
Kiwi 82, 88-89
Lemon Cheesecake 55
Licorice Stick 126
Mango 86
Maple-Walnut 129
Mocha 32
Old-Fashioned Chocolate 25, 117
Old-Fashioned Strawberry 36, 37
Old-Fashioned Vanilla 20, 21, 117
Papaya 84, 85
Peach Custard 64
Peanut Butter Banana 80
Peppermint Stick 126, 127
Pumpkin 100
Quick Vanilla 20
Ranch House Chocolate 25
Raspberry 44
Rocky Road 26, 27
Serving 13
Soft Chocolate 28
Soft Vanilla 20
Tangerine-Chip 60
Toffee-Coffee 31
Vanilla 19
Vanilla Pudding 23
Ice Cream, How to Freeze 10
Ice Cream, Making 10
Ice Cream, Ripening 12
Ice Cream, Storing 14
Ice Cream, The Story of 16
Ice
  Cantaloupe 96
  Citrus Tea 34
  Cranberry-Orange 42
  Lemon 56
  Mai Tai 90
  Minted Tea 34
  Plum Ice Italian-Style 73
  Sicilian Melon 94, 97
  Strawberry 40
  Watermelon 96
Ice, Ratios of Salt to 11
Ice, Source & Preparation of 8
Igloos, Brownie 104
Ingredients 14
Irish Coffee Ice Cream 31
Italian Cream, Strawberry 38
Italian Peach Mousse 135
Italian-Style Frozen Yogurt 22
Italian-Style, Plum Ice 73
Italiano, Hazelnut Ice Cream 124, 125

J

Jubilee, Cherries 66, 67
Junket Mix
  Heritage Peach Ice Cream 63
Just For Kids 112-120

K

Kir Spritzer, Frozen 153
Kiwi Ice Cream 82, 88-89
Kiwi Sorbet 89

L

Lemon Cheesecake Ice Cream 55
Lemon Cream, Apricot 69
Lemon Cream, Frozen 54
Lemon Cream, Magic 55
Lemon Ice 56
Lemon Sherbet 55, 108
Lemon-Lime Freeze 57
Licorice Stick Ice Cream 126
Lime Cheesecake, Frozen 111

Lime Freeze, Lemon 57
Lime Ice Cream, Dreamy 58
Lime Sherbet, Creamy 58
Loaf, Macaroon-Fudge 139

M

Macadamia Nut Ice Cream, Banana 81
Macaroon-Fudge Loaf 139
Magic Lemon Cream 55
Mai Tai Ice 90
Make-Your-Own Watermelon 138
Maker, Selecting an Ice Cream 7
Making Ice Cream 10
Mandarin-Chocolate Sherbet 30
Mandarin-Tangerine Yogurt 60
Mango Ice Cream 86
Mango Sorbet 85
Mango-Coconut Yogurt 82, 86
Maple-Walnut Ice Cream 129
Maple-Walnut Sauce 154
Mardi Gras Cream 125
Margarita Pie 102, 103
Marshmallow Sauce, Chocolate 156
Mauna Loa Topping 156
Melba Cups, Frozen 141
Melba Mold, Frozen 138
Melba, Blueberry 145
Melon Ice, Sicilian 94, 97
Melon Sorbet, Raspberry 44
Melons & Vegetables 92-100
Meringue Pie, Chocolate-Mint 105
Meringue Shells 107
Mexican Mocha Crème 33
Mincement Mousse 134
Mint Ice Cream, Chocolate Chip 26, 108
Mint Meringue Pie, Chocolate 105
Mint Truffle Mold, Chocolate 136, 137
Minted Pear Sorbet 71
Minted Tea Ice 34
Minty Grapefruit Sorbet 56, 57
Mocha Cheesecake, Frozen 111
Mocha Crème, Mexican 33
Mocha Ice Cream 32
Mocha Pie, Acapulco 102
Mold, Apricot Cream 133
Mold, Chocolate-Mint Truffle 136, 137
Mold, Frozen Melba 138
Mold, Neapolitan Cake 136
Mold, Peanut Crunch 132
Molded Frozen Desserts 131-143
Mousse Defined 16
Mousse, Burnt Almond 132, 133
Mousse, Italian Peach 135
Mousse, Mincement 134
Mousse, Royal Velvet 134
Mulled Cider Sorbet 77

N

Neapolitan Cake Mold 136
Nectarine Cream, Frozen 72
Nectarine Sorbet 72
Nut Ice Cream, Banana Macadamia 81
Nut Ice Cream, Date 90
Nut Topping, Brandied Apricot 155
Nuts, Candies & Caramels 121-130

O

Old-Fashioned Chocolate Ice Cream 25, 117
Old-Fashioned Strawberry Ice Cream 36, 37
Old-Fashioned Vanilla Ice Cream 20, 21, 117
Orange Cream Sherbet 52
Orange Cups, Avocado 52, 53
Orange Ice Cream, Avo 92
Orange Ice, Cranberry 42

Orange Pineapple Cream, Candied 126
Orange Slush 54
Orange Smoothie 148
Orange Sorbet, Banana 83
Orange Yogurt, Banana 81
Orange Yogurt, Blueberry 48
Orange Yogurt, Peachy 65
Orange-Cranberry Sherbet 43
Orange-Honey Yogurt 51, 108
Orange-Pineapple Sherbet 51, 117
Orange-Pineapple Yogurt 51
Orchard Fruits 62-78

P

Papaya Ice Cream 84, 85
Papaya, see
     Beachcomber's Delight 83
     Trade Winds Sorbet 82, 84
Parfait, Praline 145
Peach Bombe 135
Peach Custard Ice Cream 64
Peach Daiquiri, Frozen 149
Peach Ice Cream, Fresh 63
Peach Ice Cream, Heritage 63
Peach Mousse, Italian 135
Peach Sorbet 64
Peachy Orange Yogurt 65
Peanut Butter Banana Ice Cream 80
Peanut Butter Fudge Cream 25
Peanut Butter Graham Cracker
     Sandwiches 114, 115
Peanut Butter Ice Cream, Butterscotch 122
Peanut Crunch Mold 132
Peanut Crunch Topping 155
Pear Ice Cream, Ginger 70, 71
Pear Sorbet, Minted 71
Pecan Ice Cream, Butter 122
Pecan Ripple, Butterscotch 122
Peppermint Stick Ice Cream 126, 127
Pie, Acapulco Mocha 102
Pie, Chocolate-Mint Meringue 105
Pie, Frozen Eggnog-Pumpkin 103, 108
Pie, Harvey Wallbanger 104
Pie, Margarita 102, 103
Pies & Cakes 101-111
Pineapple Cream, Candied Orange 126
Pineapple Sherbet, Orange 51, 117
Pineapple Yogurt, Frozen Apricot 70
Pineapple Yogurt, Orange 51
Piña Colada, Creamy 148
Plum Ice Cream, Fresh 73
Plum Ice Italian-Style 73
Plum Sorbet, Fresh 74
Pomegranate Sorbet 74, 75
Pops, Easy Fruit 118
Pops, Fruit Salad 118, 119
Pops, Grape-Yogurt 119
Ports of Call Sorbet 91
Praline Cups 128, 129
Praline Parfait 145
Praline Sauce 154
Preparation of Ice, Source & 8
Preparing the Brine 11
Pronto Strawberry Cream 36
Pudding Ice Cream, Butterscotch 123
Pudding Ice Cream, Chocolate 29
Pudding Ice Cream, Vanilla 23
Pumpkin Ice Cream 100
Pumpkin Pie, Frozen Eggnog 103, 108
Punch Sorbet, Grape 47

Q

Quick Vanilla Ice Cream 20
Quickie Fruit Drink 148

R

Ranch House Chocolate Ice Cream 25
Raspberry Ice Cream 44
Raspberry Ice Cream, Fresh 45
Raspberry Sorbet, Tangerine 59
Raspberry Topping 155
Raspberry Yogurt Creme 44
Raspberry-Melon Sorbet 44
Ratios of Salt to Ice 11
Rhubarb Custard, Frozen 100
Rhubarb Sorbet, Strawberry 40
Ring, Banana-Brittle 139
Ring, Rocky Road Cereal 120
Ripening Ice Cream 12
Ripple Ice Cream, Fudge 28, 29
Ripple, Butterscotch-Pecan 122
Rocky Road Cereal Ring 120
Rocky Road Ice Cream 26, 27
Roll, Gingerbread 108, 110
Roll, Ice Cream 110
Royal Crown Vanilla 19
Royal Velvet Mousse 134
Rum Ice Cream, Banana 81

S

Salad Pops, Fruit 118, 119
Salt to Ice, Ratios of 11
Sandwiches, Chocolate Ice Cream 113
Sandwiches, Peanut Butter Graham
     Cracker 114, 115
Sauce, also see Syrup or Topping
Sauce, Burnt Sugar 155
Sauce, Chocolate Marshmallow 156
Sauce, Favorite Fudge 154
Sauce, Maple-Walnut 154
Sauce, Praline 154
Selecting an Ice Cream Maker 7
Serving Ice Cream 13
Shells, Meringue 107
Sherbet
     Cantaloupe 94, 95
     Coconut 87
     Creamy Lime 58
     Easy Chocolate 30
     Framboise 45
     Golden State 52
     Grape 46, 47
     Lemon 55, 108
     Mandarin-Chocolate 30
     Orange Cream 52
     Orange-Cranberry 43
     Orange-Pineapple 51, 117
     Strawberry 39
     Tangerine 61
Sicilian Melon Ice 94, 97
Silk, Green 148
Slush, Grape 46
Slush, Orange 54
Slush, Wine 152
Smoothie, Orange 148
Snowballs 120
Soda Fountain & Bar Concoctions 144-156
Soda, Strawberry 15, 146, 147
Soft Chocolate Ice Cream 28
Soft Vanilla Ice Cream 20
Sorbet
     Banana-Orange 83
     Blueberry 48
     Cantaloupe-Wine 95
     Cherry-Berry 66
     Cranberry-Wine 42, 43
     Fresh Plum 74
     Grape Punch 47
     Hawaiian 91
     Kiwi 89
     Mango 85

Index

Minted Pear 71
Minty Grapefruit 56, 57
Mulled Cider 77
Nectarine 72
Peach 64
Pomegranate 74, 75
Ports of Call 91
Raspberry-Melon 44
Strawberry 41
Strawberry-Rhubarb 40
Tangerine 61
Tangerine-Raspberry 59
Trade Winds 82, 84
Tutti Frutti 68
Watermelon 94, 97
Sorbet Defined 16
Soufflé Defined 16
Sour Cream
    Avocado-Orange Cups 52, 53
    Frozen Strawberry Sour Cream 39
    Grasshopper Ice Cream 147
    Green Chowder Frappé 100
    Orange Cream Sherbet 52
    Orange-Pineapple Sherbet 51, 117
    Spicy Applesauce Freeze 78
Source & Preparation of Ice 8
Spicy Applesauce Freeze 78
Split, Classic Banana 3-4, 145
Spritzer, Frozen Kir 153
Storing Ice Cream 14
Story of Ice Cream, The 16
Strawberry Cream 36
Strawberry Cream, Pronto 36
Strawberry Daiquiri, Frozen 149
Strawberry Ice 40
Strawberry Ice Cream, Old-Fashioned
    36, 37
Strawberry Italian Cream 38
Strawberry Sherbet 39
Strawberry Sodas 15, 146, 147
Strawberry Sorbet 41
Strawberry Sour Cream, Frozen 39
Strawberry Wine, Frozen 41

Strawberry Yogurt, Creamy 38
Strawberry Yogurt, Frozen 38
Strawberry-Rhubarb Sorbet 40
Sugar Sauce, Burnt 155
Sun-Date Yogurt 90
Sundaes, Fudge 146
Swirl, Cherry-Chocolate 68
Syrup, also see Sauce or Topping
Syrup, Coffee 156

T

Tangerine Sherbet 61
Tangerine Sorbet 61
Tangerine Yogurt, Mandarin 60
Tangerine-Chip Ice Cream 60
Tangerine-Raspberry Sorbet 59
Tea Ice Cream, Ginger 34
Tea Ice, Citrus 34
Tea Ice, Minted 34
Tea, Chocolate, Coffee & 24-34
The Story of Ice Cream 16
Toffee-Coffee Ice Cream 31
Topping, also see Sauce or Syrup
Topping, Brandied Apricot-Nut 155
Topping, Mauna Loa 156
Topping, Peanut Crunch 155
Topping, Raspberry 155
Tortoni, Wallbanger 143
Trade Winds Sorbet 82, 84
Tropical Freeze, Anytime 86
Tropical Fruits 79, 92
Truffle Mold, Chocolate-Mint 136, 137
Tutti Frutti Sorbet 68

V

Vanilla 18-23
Vanilla Ice Cream 19
Vanilla Ice Cream, Basic 19
Vanilla Ice Cream, Old-Fashioned
    20, 21, 117
Vanilla Ice Cream, Quick 20
Vanilla Ice Cream, Soft 20
Vanilla Pudding Ice Cream 23

Vanilla, Royal Crown 19
Vegetables, see Melons & Vegetables
Velvet Mousse, Royal 134

W

Wallbanger Pie, Harvey 104
Wallbanger Tortoni 143
Walnut Custard, Apple 76
Walnut Ice Cream, Maple 129
Walnut Sauce, Maple 154
Watermelon Ice 96
Watermelon Sorbet 94, 97
Watermelon, Make-Your-Own 138
Watermelon-Wine Cooler 98
Wine Slush 152
Wine Sorbet, Cantaloupe 95
Wine Sorbet, Cranberry 42, 43
Wine, Frozen Strawberry 41

Y

Yogurt
    Avocado Frozen 92
    Banana-Orange 81
    Blueberry-Orange 48
    Creamy Strawberry 38
    Frozen Apple 78
    Frozen Apricot-Pineapple 70
    Frozen Strawberry 38
    Golden Glow 99
    Grape-Yogurt Pops 119
    Italian-Style Frozen 22
    Mandarin-Tangerine 60
    Mango-Coconut 82, 86
    Orange-Honey 51, 108
    Orange-Pineapple 51
    Peachy Orange 65
    Raspberry Yogurt Creme 44
    Sun-Date 90
Yogurt, Frozen Defined 16

Z

Zabaglione, Frozen 143